AVICENNA'S
PSYCHOLOGY
A TEXTBOOK ON PERENNIAL PSYCHOLGY

LALEH BAKHTIAR

INSTITUTE OF TRADITIONAL PSYCHOLOGY

Library of Congress Cataloging-in-Publication Data

Ibn Sina, Abu Ali al-Husayn ibn Abd Allah
Psychology
    1. Psychology. 2. Medicine. I. Title

ISBN 10 (Book): 1-56744-171-8
ISBN 13 (Book): 978-1-56744-171-0

Published by
Institute of Traditional Psychology

Distributed by
KAZI Publications, Inc.
3023 W. Belmont Avenue
Chicago IL 60618
Tel: 773-267-7001; FAX: 773-267-7002
email: info@kazi.org

CONTENTS

DEDICATION

To each of the world's religious traditions
—followers of a single, universal Reality—
whose science of the soul
reflects that Reality

ACKNOWLEDGEMENTS

To my mentor, Seyyed Hossein Nasr,
To my publisher, Liaquat Ali and Kazi Publications,
To my friend Samuel Bendeck Sotillos,
To my family—

May God's blessings continue for you, forever.

EXORDIUM

AVICENNA'S ODE TO THE SOUL

It descended upon you from out of the regions above,
That exalted, ineffable, glorious, heavenly Dove.
It was concealed from the eyes of all every seeker,
Yet it wears not a veil, and is ever apparent to all.
Unwilling it sought you and joined you, and yet, though it grieve,
It is like to be still more unwilling your body to leave.
It resisted and struggled, and would not be tamed in haste,
Yet it joined them, and slowly grew used to this desolate waste,
Till, forgotten at length, as between were haunts and its troth
In the heavenly gardens and groves, which to leave it was loath.
Until, when it entered the D of its downward Descent,
And to earth, to the C of its center, unwillingly went,
The eye of (I) infirmity smote it, and lo, it was hurled
Midst the sign-posts and ruined abodes of this desolate world,
It weeps when it thinks of its home and peace it possessed,
With tears welling forth from its eyes without pausing or rest,
And with plaintive mourning it broods like one bereft
Over such trace of its home as the fourfold winds have left.
Thick nets detain it, and strong is the case whereby
It is held from seeking the lofty and spacious sky,
Until, when the hour of its homeward flight draws near,
And it is time for it to return to its ampler sphere,
It carols with joy, for the veil is raised, and it spies
Such things as cannot be witnessed by waking eyes.
On a lofty height it warbles its songs of praise
(For even the lowliest being does knowledge raise).
And so it returns, aware of all hidden things
In the universe, while no stain to its garment clings.

Now why from its perch on high was it cast like this
To the lowest Nadir's gloomy and dear abyss?
Was it God who cast it forth for some purpose wise,
Concealed from the keenest seeker's inquiring eyes?
Then in its descent a discipline wise but stern,
That the things that it had not heard it thus may learn.
So it is it whom fate plunders, while its star
Sets at length in a place from its rising far,

Like a gleam of lightning which over the meadows shone,
And, as though it never had been, in a moment is gone.[1]

In the Name of God, the Merciful, the Compassionate

AUTHOR'S PREFACE

BIOGRAPHICAL SKETCH OF AVICENNA

For a biographical sketch of Avicenna and his works, we turn to a great contemporary Avicennian scholar and philosopher, Seyyed Hossein Nasr:

Abu Ali Sina, known to the Western world as Avicenna and entitled "the Prince of Physicians," was born in 370/980 near Bukhara. The sage who was later to become the most influential of all figures in the Islamic arts and sciences and who was to gain such titles as al-Shaikh al-rais (the Leader among Wise Men) and Hujjat al-Haqq (the Proof of God), by which he is still known in the East, displayed a remarkable aptitude for learning from an early age. He was also fortunate in that his father, an Ismaili, took great interest in his education and that his house was a meeting place for scholars from near and far. Avicenna learned the whole of the Quran, as well as grammar, by the age of ten and then undertook to study logic and mathematics, the latter under the direction of Abu Abdullah al-Natili. Having rapidly mastered these subjects he then undertook a study of physics, metaphysics, and medicine with Abu Sahl al-Masili. At the age of sixteen he was the master of all the sciences of his day except for metaphysics as contained in the *Metaphysics* of Aristotle which, though he had read it over many times and even memorized it, he could not understand. But even this obstacle was removed when he discovered by chance the commentary of al-Farabi upon the work which clarified all its difficult points for him. From then on Avicenna had nothing more to learn 'in breadth' but needed only to increase his understanding 'in depth' of what he had already learned by the time he was eighteen years old. In fact, toward the twilight of his life he once mentioned to his favorite disciple, al-Juzjani, that in all the intervening years he had learned no more than he knew as a youth of eighteen.

Avicenna's mastery of medicine had already made him a favorite of the ruler. The doors of the palace library were opened to him and he enjoyed a reputable position at court. But the pressure of political turmoil in Central Asia caused by the growing power of Mahmud of Ghazna was making life difficult and unstable in his home province and eventually forced Avicenna to abandon Bukhara for Jurjaniyah and finally leave that region altogether for Jurjan. In 403/1012, amidst great hardship, in which several of his companions perished, Avicenna crossed the desert to Khurasan. According to most traditional authorities, he visited the famous Sufi saint and poet, Abu Said ibn Abil-Khair, before reaching Jurjan, where he hoped to meet the famous patron of the arts, Qabus ibn Wush-mgir. But upon arrival he discovered that his would-be patron had already died.

Disappointed by this misfortune, he retired to a village for a few years and then left for Rai sometime between 405/1014 and 406/1015. At this time Persia was under the control of the Buyid dynasty, various members of which ruled over the different provinces of the country. Avicenna spent some time at the court of Fakhr al-Dawlah in Rai and then set out for Hamadan to meet another member of this dynasty, Shams al-Dawlah. This meeting was made easy, for soon after his arrival in that city he was asked to treat the ruler, who had become ill. Shams al-Dawlah recovered, and Avicenna became so great a favorite at court that he was finally made a minister, a position whose heavy duties he performed for several years until the ruler's death. Then his political fortunes took a bad turn and upon his refusal to continue as minister he was imprisoned and could only escape by taking advantage of a siege of Hamadan, and then incognito in the dress of a dervish.

Having freed himself at last from his involvements in Hamadan, Avicenna set out for Ispahan, which, as a great center of learning, he had wanted to visit for many years. In Isfahan he came to the attention of Ala al-Dawlah and enjoyed a long period of peace in that city which lasted fifteen years. During that time he wrote many important works and even began to study astronomy and to construct an observatory. However, even this peaceful interim in a tumultuous life was interrupted by the invasion of lsfahan by Masud, the son of Mahmud of Ghazna, who had forced Avicenna to leave his original abode in his youth—an invasion which caused many of the sage's works to be lost. Deeply disturbed by these conditions and suffering also from an attack of colic, he returned once again to Hamadan where he died in 428/1037 and where his tomb is to be found today.

Thus ended a life which saw many political upheavals and was itself marked by many difficulties. Avicenna experienced numerous ups and downs in life, numerous happy days, but some difficult and trying ones as well. He acted most often as a physician to various princes and so led a very active social life. On occasion he even had to accept the responsibility of running a state. Yet he lived at the same time an intense intellectual life, as witnessed by the number and nature of his works and the quality of his students. He was a man of great physical power, spending long nights in gay festivities and going on from there to write a treatise on some question of philosophy or science.* (Note re wine, women) He was also a man of remarkable concentrative powers, dictating some of his works to a scribe while riding on horseback with the king to a battle. In fact none of the external disturbances of the world seems to have affected his intellectual output. The man who was so immersed in the life of the world in both politics and at court was also able to lay the foundation of medieval scholastic philosophy, to synthesize the Hippocratic and Galenic traditions of medicine, and to influence the Islamic arts and sciences in a way which no other figure has ever been able to do before or after him.[2]

THE AVICENNIAN CORPUS
ON PSYCHOLOGY

Avicenna's psychology deals with "self" as body, soul and spirit. His writings on psychology include philosophical, ethical and medical works.

In Persian, there is his *Danishnamah-i alai* (The Book of Science Dedicated to Ala al-Dawlah) and his *Risalah dar haqiqat wa kaifiyat*. In Arabic there is his *Kitab al-najat* (*The Book of Salvation*), the section on psychology translated by Fazlur Rahman under the title *Avicenna's Psychology*.

Avicenna's writing on psychology in his *Kitab al-najat* is essentially a short philosophical treatise containing proofs of the existence of the soul and not psychology, as such, as found in this present work under the same English title.

Avicenna's work entitled *al-Adwiyyah al-qalbiyyah* (Latin *De viribus cordis*) is a treatise on psychology. He also wrote briefly on psychology in his *Kitab al-isharat wa tanbihat* (Book on Directives and Remarks), *Fil ilm al-nafs* (*On the Science of the Soul: A Synopsis*), *Fil birr wal ithm* (Piety and Sin), *Fil al-ilm al-akhlaq* (On the Science of Ethics) in *Tis rasail fil hikmah wal tabiyyah, Ahwal al-nafs, Fil akhlaq wal infialat al-nafsaniyyah* and *Fil ahd in Tis rasail fil hikmah wal tabiyyah*.

The best source, however, for Avicenna's psychology is his work on medicine including his *Urjuzah fil tibb* (*Poem on Medicine*) and, particularly, his five volume work, *The Canon of Medicine* (*TCM*).

His *Poem on Medicine* is a summary of *The Canon*. Physicians were offered a mnemonic in the form of a poem which established the essentials of Avicenna's theory and practice.

To recognize the importance of his *Canon* for understanding his psychology, it is helpful to learn something of the background of *The Canon of Medicine* that was written somewhere around 1030 CE.

In general, Avicenna derives his system of medicine from that of the Graeco-Roman physician Galen (120-200 CE) who himself took Hippocratic medicine as his starting point. Avicenna additionally augments his Greek medical and anatomical sources with developments made by physicians in Islamic lands, such as those of Abu Bakr ar-Razi (the Latin

Rhazes; 865-925 or 932) and Ali ibn al-Abbas al-Majusli (the Latin Haly Abbas; d. ca. 990). . . .[3]

It is important to remember in this regard:

> Muslims did adopt much of Greek medicine, especially its theory, but this adoption was possible only because of the traditional nature of this medicine and its concordance with the Islamic conception of the Universe. It must not be forgotten that here as in the domain of philosophy the Muslims considered the origin of this science to be prophetic and sacred and in fact related to the Abrahamic prophetic chain which the Muslims considered to be their own.
>
> The rapid assimilation of Greek medical theory into the Islamic perspective is due most of all to this latent possibility within the Islamic perspective itself and the close relation between the idea of the harmony of parts in Hippocratic and Galenic medicine and the concept of balance and harmony so central to Islam. It is not accidental that the theoretical background of Greek medicine belongs to the same schools of Greek philosophy which were easily assimilated into the Islamic perspective and not to those which the Muslims rejected.
>
> The reasons for the 'Muslimization' of a Hippocrates or Galen are nearly the same as those of a Plato or an Aristotle and are also related to the reasons for the rejection of other schools of Greek thought, such as the Epicurean or the Sophist. Had Greek medicine possessed a theoretical background related to the anti-metaphysical schools of late Antiquity, it is very doubtful whether it would have been integrated so perfectly within the Islamic intellectual universe.[4]

Why was Avicenna's *Canon of Medicine* practiced through his medical textbook for almost 700 years in Europe? Why was this Muslim practitioner favored over the works of the Greeks?

> While it is true that Avicenna's system of medicine in the main is derivative, namely, an amalgamation of Aristotle, Galen, and others, it would be wrong on that account to dismiss it as not being of historical, philosophical, and scientific interest and importance in its own right. First, Galen's own medical and philosophical corpus extends to twenty volumes in its modern edition, which itself does not include some treatises that are only extant in Arabic translation. Consequently, given the extent of his writings, mastering Galen's corpus was a tedious and painstaking enterprise for the medieval [practitioner]. Moreover, since few [practitioners] would be able to possess the complete Galenic opera, they were often without any practical reference work of medicine. Thus, Avicenna's com-

paratively short five-volume *The Canon of Medicine* was a godsend for later physicians, whether as an introductory textbook for those just beginning to study the art of medicine or as a relatively concise and easily manageable handbook of the best medicine at the time for the seasoned doctor.[5]

In addition, throughout these centuries, *The Canon of Medicine* was translated into Persian, Chinese, Hebrew, German, French as well as Latin. The entire five volumes of *The Canon* was first translated into Latin by Gerard of Cremona in the 12th century. English translations began in the 1930s with O. Cameron Gruner's translation of volume 1 based on the Latin translations produced in Venice in 1595 and 1608 CE supported by a study of the Arabic edition printed in Rome in 1593 and the Bulaq edition.[6]

The original publication of the English translation by Gruner, remarkable as it is because of Gruner's extensive notes, was difficult to distinguish between what Avicenna wrote and Gruner's notes. In addition, Gruner did not include Avicenna's chapter on anatomy. The author of this present work on *Avicenna's Psychology* then adapted Gruner's translation and that of the translation in 1964 by M. H. Shah, in particular, Avicenna's chapter on anatomy supported by a study of the Persian translation and Arabic original.

In addition, Gruner added a translation of Avicenna's *al-Adwiyya al-qalbiyya* to his translation of Volume 1 of *The Canon*. This is not in Avicenna's *Canon*, but a separate treatise, nor in the Shah translation nor a later English translation published in 1993 by Jamia Hamdard.

For the available adaptation of *The Canon of Medicine*, Volume 1, by this author, there was no access to the extremely limited printing and only local distribution of the Jamia Hamdard translation. Since the publication of this adaptation, the present author has also adapted Volume 2 of *The Canon: On Natural Pharmaceuticals* which is available and is in the process of finalizing the translation of the other volumes.

There are two different views on why *The Canon* became the most important medical textbook in Europe for all these centuries. The first is the view of Jon McGinnis. He writes that an important note in regard to the importance of Avicenna's medical writing that incudes his treatment of psychology and how it affects the body in order that a person be treated in a holistic way:

> . . .is that when Galen himself was writing, the Neoplatonized Aristotelianism that would emerge in Alexandria as the dominant philosophical system during the Middle Ages in the Islamic world had not yet been developed. Indeed, Aristotelianism at Galen's time was in genuine com-

petition with such philosophical schools as Skepticism, Stoicism, and Middle Platonism. Galen himself in fact preferred Stoic materialism as the underlying physics for his medical theory, a theory, one might add, that viewed the human soul as a subtle material substance and so was diametrically opposed to the immaterialist view that Avicenna espoused in his psychology. As a consequence, in Avicenna's day there was something of a scientific crisis at least for philosophers, for the best medicine of the time was based on a materialism that was at odds with what was believed to be the best physical and psychological theories of the time. It is thus no wonder that a continuing theme in Avicenna's medical writing was to retain as much of Galen's humoural medical theory as was possible, while protecting Avicenna's own preferred doctrine of an immaterial human [soul and] intellect from Galenic subversion.[7]

Whoever reads and studies *The Canon of Medicine* cannot fail to be impressed with the way Avicenna was able to integrate his medicine as part and parcel of his scientific and philosophical works.

> Time and time again, Avicenna easily resolves thorny technical issues in medicine simply by referring the reader to his philosophical discussions in his works on physics, biology, and even metaphysics. The importance, then, of *The Canon*, and indeed Avicenna's medical writings more generally, is that it formed an integral part of a medieval world view that incorporated and explained virtually every area of human intellectual pursuit. . . .[8]

The second view in regard to the success of *The Canon* in Europe from the 13th to the 18th centuries is found in the *Encyclopedia Iranica*:

> [*The Canon of Medicine*] met the needs of the new scholastic medicine in three respects: (1) with its immense wealth of information, it provided Western practitioners with a synopsis of virtually all the knowledge amassed in the preceding 1500 years [500 BCE-1000 CE] and stimulated them to work further on their own; (2) with its systematic incorporation of every subject, down to the smallest detail, in a well-ordered theoretical framework, it greatly facilitated the adoption of its contents for teaching and at the same time satisfied the scholastic liking for a logical classification of subject matter; (3) last but not least, Avicenna linked the medicine of Galen to the natural philosophy and theory of science of Aristotle, Aristotelian views on basic questions of biology (e.g., the central organ of the body, the roles of the sexes in reproduction) provided starting points for discussions, typical of the scholastic medicine of the time, about the discrepancies between philosophers and practitioners, i.e., between Ar-

istotle and Galen, and thereby prompted new efforts to solve old problems.[9]

When one understands Avicenna's view on the connection of the soul to the body, one learns that it is, in fact, the soul (*psyche, anima, nafs*) that enlivens the body to then creates a living being.

Among the later philosophers and scientists, Christian and Jewish, perhaps the most important historic figure who was immensely influenced by Avicenna was Thomas Aquinas and scholastic philosophy. Aquinas often quoted Avicenna more often than Aristotle and is reported to have said: Whatever Avicenna says is true.

Among the contributions of Avicenna to psychology and psychotherapy are his noting "the close relationship between emotions and the physical condition of a patient" and music that "had a definite physical and psychological effect on patients."[10]

When describing the theory of the four temperaments, Avicenna extended it to encompass "emotional aspects, mental capacity, moral attitudes, self-awareness, movements and dreams."[11]

"In clinical psychology and psychotherapy, Avicenna often used psychological methods to treat his patients.[12]

"Avicenna was to discover psychophysiology and psychosomatic medicine and the first to recognize physiological psychology in the treatment of disorders involving emotions and developed a system for associating changes in the pulse rate with inner feelings, which is seen as an anticipation of the word association test attributed to Carl Jung. Avicenna describes melancholia (depression) as a type of mood disorder in which the person may become suspicious and develop certain types of phobias. It stated that anger heralded the transition of melancholia to mania and explained that humidity inside the head can contribute to mood disorders. It recognized that this occurs when the amount of vital energy changes: happiness increases the vital energy [in the heart] which leads to increased moisture inside the brain [nervous energy], but if this moisture goes beyond its limits, the brain would lose control over its rationality and lead to mental disorders. He also described symptoms and treatments for nightmare, epilepsy and weak memory."[13]

AVICENNA'S PSYCHOLOGY

In regard to the science of psychology, Avicenna is most interested in investigating the causes of changes in living bodies and the activities in which they engage. He reasons that living bodies that can move of their own will must have come cause that distinguishes them from things that do not move from their own volition.

He searched for the cause:

> The science of psychology is primarily interested in the cause (or causes) belonging to living bodies that explains that set of activities unique to them as living. Thus, in I.1 of the [*Kitab al-Shifa*], Psychology, Avicenna begins by pointing out that it is simply a matter of empirical observation that certain bodies sensibly perceive and move about voluntarily, as well as taking in nourishment, growing, and reproducing.
>
> These activities, he continues, cannot belong to them simply inasmuch as they are bodies, for otherwise all bodies would manifest these activities, which they clearly do not.
>
> A stone may be split in two or fall to the ground, but no one would say that in such cases it has reproduced or moved around of its own will. Given this difference between the natural activities of different kinds of bodies, living bodies must have some other principle or cause in addition to their mere corporeality.[14]

For Avicenna, the word "soul" is simply

> . . . .a word to indicate that thing or things, whatever it or they might be, that living bodies have that non-living bodies lack and on account of which living bodies do those activities that define them as living.[15]

The soul is known by observing change:

> . . . .we may not know what the soul is, but we know it exists, because we can see what it does. Medicine can also reveal other truths about the soul, such as the location of its various parts in the brain, heart and liver, or its transmission through the nerves. Different aspects of the soul exhibit different 'powers', i.e., causal postulates conceived in relation to their specific effects. Thus the soul can be a proper object of scientific inquiry if one concentrates on its evident manifestations, and seeks to make causal and categorical sense of them within a general theory of functioning.[16]

NATURAL SCIENCE

Avicenna's Natural Science included the study of the bodies of which the universe is composed: the heavens and the stars in the macrocosm and the simple elements of earth, air, fire and water and their elemental properties of hot, cold, moist and dry as well as the compound bodies of minerals, plants, animals and human beings; how they change, develop and intermix.

> Natural [Science] is that aspect of wisdom which deals with the domain that moves and changes. It is the study, at once quantitative and qualitative, of that which is an accident and constitutes, along with mathematics and metaphysics, the domain of [theoretical] philosophy. The branches of natural philosophy constitute all the sciences of the sublunary region [the world of generation and corruption] including that of the sciences of medicine, [psychology and ethics].[17]

For Avicenna, the human being is a microcosm of the macrocosmic universe. As with other traditional scientists, he follows two cardinal doctrines:

> . . . .namely the hierarchic structure of the cosmos and the correspondence between the microcosm and the macrocosm.[18]

In his view, the human body is the instrument used by the soul and the spirit that make up the human being's inner world connecting them outwardly through the grades of the hierarchy of the macrocosm back to the Source of cosmic manifestation.

> Likewise they sought the principles of medicine [and psychology] in the sciences dealing with the Principle and its manifestations, namely metaphysics and cosmology. Whatever may have been the historical origins of Islamic medicine, its principles cannot be understood save in the light of Islamic metaphysics and cosmological sciences.[19]

THE WORLD OF GENERATION AND CORRUPTION

The unfolding of the human soul in the world of generation and corruption begins with the role of the four elements and their elemental properties in creating 'matter".

> [The world of generation and corruption is] a world in which the soul and matter are united empowering living objects at various levels. In contrast to the heavens where separate things like the intelligences or angels can exist without matter, the condition of existence in the sublunary world requires the existence of matter for every form and form for all matter.

In fact, it is this necessity that causes continuous change.[20]

According to Avicenna, each body acquires a particular soul and every soul in-forms a particular body. This, then, gives the soul its particular individuality as every living object is "in-formed" matter. Human nature is in-formed matter, bearing certain properties or marks and endowed with existence. Each organ in the body is in-formed matter. Every tissue is informed matter. The blood, the lymph, the urine, etc, are each of them informed matter. Every microscopic cell of which the tissues are composed is merely in-formed matter. So also is every chemical entity which composes the cells, and the whole person also is just in-formed matter.

As a result of the movement of the forces of nature in the sublunar region, Avicenna explains:

. . . .a great deal of heat was generated, and from the heat the separation of the [elements] of this region was brought about. The separation in turn caused dryness; hence a substance called fire, possessing the qualities of heat and dryness, came into being. Whatever remained of the [remaining elements] fell away from the heavens toward the center. Unable to move, it became cold; the cold quality caused opaqueness and subsequently dryness.

Out of these qualities of dryness and cold, the element earth was formed. Whatever of the [elements] remained was bound by the earth below and fire above. The half near the fire became warm without there being any separation among its parts since the heat was not excessive. Therefore, a new element comprised of the qualities of heat and moisture called air, came into being. The other half near the earth became cold, but since this coldness was not excessive, it did not condense, so that an element consisting of the qualities of moisture and cold, called water, was formed. In this way the four principles of all sublunary bodies were generated.

The progressive 'coagulation' of the [elements] terminates with extreme differentiation, and the process of emanation reaches its terminal point. Henceforth the movement is no longer a drawing away from the principle but a return to it, not an emanation, but a love, by which all things are attracted to the source of all Being.

The elements in mixing together reach a degree of harmony which permits the descent of the lowest form of soul upon them. This descent brings into being the minerals [enlivened by the mineral soul and the power to preserve forms. This is] the lowest kingdom of the physical domain. In the mineral kingdom itself, subtleness increases until in the jewels, the highest members of this domain, the 'fire of the soul' is much stronger than in stones or mud.

In the coral, the first stage of the plant kingdom is reached [enlivened by the plant or vegetative soul and the powers of self-nourishment, growth and reproduction]. The increase in [perfection] of the mixture of elements permits a new soul, or more precisely a new [power] of the soul to descend upon it. This new [power], and not the elements or their manner of combination, is responsible for the characteristics that distinguish the plant world from the mineral. In the plant kingdom, also, there is a hierarchy in which [perfection] increases, reaching its highest degree in the palm tree, which already possesses certain features of animals.

With increasing [perfection] in the mixing of the elements, again a new [power] of the soul—this time called the animal soul [and the powers of motivation and sensation/perception]—enters the stage of the cosmic play and manifests itself in ever greater degree from the snail to the monkey, which even resembles the human being in certain of his features.

The hierarchy of being rises with the degree of [perfection] to the stages of the human being. . . . In each case a new soul or [the power] of the soul comes into play. There are also stages above that of humanity, including the stage of the spiritual soul through which the Active Intellect is reached, and finally the highest stage, that of the saints and prophets, which itself comprises numerous angelic worlds. *There is not any of us but he has a known station.* (Q37:164)

The end of the whole cosmic process is [God] from whom all things began. Creation therefore comes from God and returns to Him. *Say: God guides to the Truth. Has not He who guides to The Truth a better right to be followed than he who guides not unless he himself be guided? What is the matter with you? How you give judgment!* (Q10:35) *And to Him the whole matter will be returned.*[21]

THE FOUR CAUSES

Avicenna advises the psychologist as well as the medical doctor that they should be aware of the four causes: Material, Formal, Efficient and Final and what constitutes each cause.

He lists the things that a practitioner should accept without proof and recognize as being true as being: (1) the elements and their number; (2) the existence of temperament and its varieties; (3) humours, their number and location; (4) powers of the soul, their number and location; (5) Breath of Life and Innate Heat, their number and location; and (6) the general law that a state cannot exist without a cause and the four causes.

Things which have to be inferred and proved by reason are: (1) disorders; (2) their causes; (3) symptoms; (4) treatment; and (5) their appropriate methods of prevention. Some of these matters have to be fully explained by reason in reference to both amount (*miqdar*) and time (*waqt*).

The practitioner must also know how to arrive at conclusions concerning: (1) the causes of disorders [of the body or soul] and the individual signs thereof; and (2) the method most likely to remove the disorders and so restore health. Wherever they are obscure, he must be able to assign to them their duration, and recognize their phases.[22]

CONCLUSION

To summarize Avicenna's psychology, we could outline it in the following way, the details of which will follow through the chapters of this work:

It is here in the sublunary world that the Giver of Forms, a separate intelligence and an immaterial substance, gives substantial forms to properly prepared primary matter. The properly prepared primary matter of living bodies (other than the human being) consists of the elements and their elemental qualities. The properly prepared primary matter that will take on a human form consists of undifferentiated humours (the humours playing the basic role within the human form similar to the role of the elements in the sublunary world).

When the human male and female ova unite in creating an embryo, the embryo receives the substantial form of the human soul from the Giver of Forms. The Giver of Forms activates the Breath of Life (Spirit), Innate Heat and Radical Moisture from the undifferentiated humour.

> God also created the Breath of Life to enable the powers of the soul to be conveyed into the corresponding organs and members. In the first place the Breath of Life was to be the rallying point for the powers of the soul, and in the second place it was to be an emanation (through its energies that, when activated, become powers of the soul) into the various members and tissues of the body.
>
> He produced the Breath of Life out of the finer particles of the humours, and out of fieriness; and, at the same time, produced the tissues themselves out of the coarser and earthy particles of these humours. In other words, the Breath of Life is related to the thinner particles as the body is related to the coarser particles of the same humours.
>
> The beginning of the Breath of Life is as a divine emanation from potentiality to actuality proceeding without intermission or stint until the form is completed and perfected.[23]

The Breath of Life enters the heart where it undergoes combustion and circulates throughout the embryo through its blood stream.

The Breath of Life produces three energies (spirits): vital, natural and nervous. The vital energy enters the heart; the natural energy enters the liver; and the nervous energy enters the brain. These three energies cause the humours to separate into the four humours. Each of the humours has a pair of the elemental qualities (fire: hot and dry; air: hot and wet; water: cold and wet; earth: cold and dry) that form the temperament of the body. These three energies activate the powers (faculties) of the human soul.

The human soul includes: the power of the mineral soul to preserve shape or form; the powers of the vegetal or plant soul of growth, reproduction and nutrition and nutrition's four secondary powers of attraction, digestion, retention and evacuation; and the powers of the animal soul.

The powers of the animal soul includes the power of motion/motivation and the power of sensation/perception. The power of motivation along with the power of motion includes the concupiscent and the irascible powers, the latter two known as "the passions." The animal soul power of sensation/perception includes the powers of sensation: the five external powers of seeing, hearing, smelling, tasting and touching. The powers of perception include the five internal powers: common sense, retention, estimation, memory and imagination. Imagination divides into two powers: sensitive (all animals) and rational (human being only).

When speaking about the powers that use the body as its instrument to effect change, motion or motivation, the word "soul" is used. When the soul's powers are involved with intellection and estimation, they are called "intellects" as the soul is potentially "intellect." When the intellect receives intuitive illumination, it is called the "spiritual" heart, intellect or soul.

The rational intellect is divided into two parts: the theoretical intellect and the practical intellect. The theoretical intellect has four levels— material, habitual, actual and acquired intellects. The acquired intellect can ascend to the level of the spiritual soul/intellect that is that of the prophets and saints. The theoretical intellect, directed upwards to receive intelligibles, is activated by the Active Intellect (the Active Intellect is to intelligibles what the Giver of Forms is to forms). The practical intellect, directed downwards and under the direction of the theoretical intellect, governs the body.

As only the human soul is rational and contains all of the powers of the soul, it is considered to be potentially the soul in its most complete and perfect form. This is why Rumi can speak of the various grades of the soul moving towards completion and perfection. In other words, it is the soul within living beings that causes change as Rumi indicates:

I died from mineral and plant became;
Died from the plant and took a sentient frame;
Died from the beast and donned a human dress;
When by my dying did I e'er grow less:
Another time from manhood I must die
To soar with angel-pinions through the sky.
'Midst angels also I must lose my place.
Since 'Everything shall perish save His Face.'
Let me be Naught! The harp-strings tell me plain
That unto Him do we return again![24]

The major roles of the rational intellect, also known as reason, is to control the irrational animal powers known as the passions: concupiscence (attraction to pleasure, lust) and irascibility (avoidance of harm/pain, anger). The struggle of reason with the passions is considered by Avicenna to be the Final Cause of the Soul.

*****

This work is divided into three parts:

Part One: The Morphology of the Soul introduces the soul and its various manifestations including the mineral, plant, animal and human souls/intellects.

Part Two: The Causes of the Soul, the first being the Material, includes the Four Elements, the Four Humours, the Organs and the Temperament and elemental qualities.

The Formal Cause includes the Giver of Forms/Active Intellect, the Energies of the Spirit including the Breath of Life, Innate Heat and Radical Moisture and the Powers of the Soul.

The Efficient Cause develops the six major categories of external causes that affect the soul: Air; Dietetics, Food and Drink; Exercise, Rest and Massage; Sleep and Wakefulness; Psychological Factors; and Retention and Evacuation.

Part Three: The Final Cause: Completing and Perfecting the Soul. The purpose of the soul is to complete and perfect itself. This is done through moral healing as Avicenna states in his treatise on ethics (*Fil al-ilm al-akhlaq*). According to Avicenna and the psychology of others such as al-Kindi, ibn Miskaywah, al-Farabi and al-Ghazzali, the goal of the soul is to attain completion and perfection through moral healing.

Part Four: Conclusion. Critical Thinking.

All references to *The Canon of Medicine* (*TCM*) are references to Volume 1.

PART ONE:
ON THE MORPHOLOGY OF THE SOUL
CHAPTER 1 ON THE SOUL

The soul is the governor of the body. It is immaterial and indivisible. The soul is that which enlivens the body when its powers are activated by the energies of the Breath of Life to perform its various activities whether the body be asleep or not sensing or not moving. It cannot be measured in terms of space or time or of quantity.

THE BODY IS THE INSTRUMENT OF THE SOUL

The soul comes into existence whenever a body does so fit to be used by it. The body which thus comes into being is the kingdom and instrument of the soul. In the very disposition of the substance of the soul which comes into existence together with a certain body—a body, that is to say, with the appropriate qualities to make it suitable to receive the soul which takes its origin from the first principles—there is a natural inclination or yearning to occupy itself with that body, to use it, control it, and be attracted by it.[25]

Avicenna states that there is no transmigration of the soul from one body to another as each soul is unique to each body. If there were to be transmigration of the soul, the new body would have its own soul and the previous body, its soul. One body cannot have two souls:

We have said before that the couplement of a soul with a body is not a matter of mere chance so that souls exist on their own account independent of bodies and organized bodies exist apart from souls and then souls come to inhabit bodies by chance. On the contrary, every organized body requires a particular soul. Now, if we suppose a soul that transmigrates from one body into another, the second body will have two souls— one its own soul, since being an organized body it must require a particular soul of its own, and the other which will transmigrate into it from another body. This is absurd. Therefore, there cannot be any transmigration of souls.[26]

THE SOUL YEARNS FOR UNION

This inclination or yearning binds the soul specially to this body, and turns it away from other bodies different from it in nature so that the soul does not contact them except through it. Thus when the principle of its individualization, namely, its peculiar dispositions, occurs to it, it becomes an individual. These dispositions determine its attachment to that particular body and form the relationship of their mutual suitability, although this relationship and its condition may be obscure to us.[27]

> All the four elements are seething in this caldron (the world),
> None is at rest, neither earth nor fire nor water nor air.
> Now earth takes the form of grass, on account of desire,
> Now water becomes air, for the sake of this affinity.
> By way of unity, water becomes fire.
> Fire also becomes air in this expanse by reason of love.
> The elements wander from place to place like a pawn,
> For the sake of the king's love, not, like you, for pastime.[28]

THE SOUL ENSOULS THE BODY

The soul achieves its first actuality (Breath of Life that directs an organism toward self-fulfillment) through the body. The subsequent development of the soul, however, does not depend on the body but on its own nature.[29]

THE SOUL IS A UNITY
BUT IN-FORMS IN DIFFERENT WAYS

An objection may be raised against our doctrine of the unity of the soul. The objection is that in plants we find only the vegetative soul and not the animal and rational souls, while in animals we find the first two only to the exclusion of the third. This suggests that each of these is an independent soul and that the soul is not one whole. The answer to this is that the soul is a unity but that certain bodies are unfit, through lack of proper temperament, to receive the whole soul and therefore receive only a part.

To give a physical analogy, fire is one unitary substance but may warm or illuminate or engender a flame in an object according to the capacity and position of the object. Warmth alone or warmth and illumination together may exist without the flame, but when the flame exists, the former two will automatically exist along with it. Each subsequent state will automatically exist along with it. Each subsequent state includes the former and transcends it. . . .[30]

MATTER AND PERFECTION

Avicenna prefers to use the terms "matter" for the body and "perfection" for the soul rather than the Aristotelian "form" for the soul. He explains:

> While every form is a perfection, not every perfection is a form. For the ruler is a perfection of the city and the captain is a perfection of the ship, but they are not respectively a form of the city and form of the ship. So whatever perfection that is itself separate is not in fact the form belonging to matter and in the matter, since the form that is in the matter is the form imprinted in it and subsisting through it.[31]

Avicenna defines "soul," saying: "The soul is the first **perfection** of a natural body that has organs that performs the activities of life."[32]

He distinguishes between two perfections. The first, presented above, is that by which a species becomes a species such as the sword's shape. The second perfection is whatever follows after this, that is, its abilities or activities, actions and passions such as a sword's ability to cut.[33]

According to Avicenna, a living body (consisting of material or physical shape or matter and the its perfection or immaterial soul and spirit) perform certain functions or activities that sets it apart from non-living bodies.

CHAPTER 2 THE MANIFESTATIONS OF THE SOUL

THE MINERAL SOUL

When the qualities of the four elements mix to a certain proportion, they receive the mineral soul. The mineral soul has the function of preserving forms. It is attached to the mixture of the qualities.

> From this wedding [of the elemental qualities] results the formation of the lowest domain of beings on earth consisting of the whole of the mineral kingdom.
>
> Avicenna adopts the Aristotelian vapor and exhalation theory to explain the formation of the mineral world. Exhalations and vapors locked up inside the earth become the cause of minerals. Each mineral contains some amount of the exhalation or vapor and different proportions of the four qualities. In some minerals, sulphur and salammoniac, for example, the exhalation exceeds, while in beryl and rubies, the vapor is dominant. Precious stones are formed also from exhalations and vapors that fall under the influence of the stars. . .
>
> [Avicenna] divides minerals into four groups: stones, fusible substances, sulphurs and salts. The difference in them is due to the difference in the strength of the substance from which they are made. For example: The material of malleable bodies is a moist substance united so firmly with the coldness and moisture of an earthy substance that the two cannot be separated from one another. The moist substance has been congealed by cold after heat has acted upon it and matured it.[34]

THE VEGETATIVE OR PLANT SOUL

In addition to the function of the mineral soul to preserve forms, plants receive three functions of the soul: nutrition, growth and reproduction. Avicenna says regarding the vegetative or plant soul:

> When the elements are mixed together in a more harmonious way, i.e., in a more balanced proportion than in the case [of minerals], other beings also come into existence out of them due to the energies of the heavenly bodies creating plants. Now some plants are grown from seed and set aside a part of the body bearing the reproductive ability or power, while others grow from spontaneous generation without seeds.
>
> The soul is like a single genus divisible in some way into three parts. The plant soul is the first actuality [or Breath of Life that directs an organ-

ism toward self-fulfillment] of an elementary natural body [consisting of the four elements and their qualities] that potentially possesses life and which is the instrument of the soul in so far as it reproduces, grows and assimilates nourishment. Food is a body whose function it is to become similar to the nature of the body whose food it is said to be, and adds to that body either in exact proportion or more or less what is dissolved. . . .

Since plants nourish themselves, the plant soul functions to provide nutrition. And because it is of the nature of plants to grow, it follows that they contain the function for growth. Again, since it is the nature of certain plants to reproduce their like and to be reproduced by their like, they contain the function of reproduction.

Unripe fruits possess the nutritive, but not the reproductive source of energy, just as they possess the power for growth but not that of reproduction. Similarly, the power for nutrition differs from that of growth. Do you not see that decrepit animals have the nutritive ability or power but lack that of growth?[35]

In addition to the physiological aspects of the plant soul, one must also consider:

Plants have certain parts, like roots, whose function is to maintain plant life, but also certain features such as beautiful patterns and colors, symmetry and smell, which are created to be appreciated and contemplated by beings other than the plants and by [ability or powers] both sensual and intellectual that the plants themselves do not possess.[36]

THE ANIMAL SOUL

The functions of the plant soul also exist in the animal species in general, not in their specific sense, the animal soul having a higher degree of perfection than that of the vegetative or plant soul.

When the moisture of the elements approaches even closer to balance, equilibrium, the animal soul becomes attached to it. The animal, besides having the potential functions of the minerals and plants, possesses additional [functions] that it gains by virtue of the coming into play of this new soul.[37]

Avicenna further explains the animal soul:

The next is the animal soul, which is the actuality [a Breath of Life that directs an organism toward self-fulfillment] of an elementary natural body that potentially possesses life and which is the instrument of the soul in so far as it moves by its will and perceives individuals.

The animal soul emerges from a compound of elements [hot, cold, moist, dry] whose organic nature is much nearer to the mean than the previous two and is, therefore, prepared to receive the animal soul, having passed through the stages of the mineral and plant soul. And so the nearer it approachs the mean, the greater is its capacity for receiving yet another power, more refined than the previous one.

According to the primary division, the animal soul has the powers of motivation and sensation/perception.[38]

THE HUMAN RATIONAL SOUL/INTELLECT

The human being shares the animal soul of animals as well as the plant and mineral souls of the respective species. In addition, its functions include motion/motivation, free will and cognition that are part of the human or rational soul or intellect.

The human rational soul/intellect is a substance that is the very essence of what it is to be a human being. It is because of the human soul/intellect that we are able to understand ideas and intelligibles by observing the effects and activities that originate in the rational soul/intellect and to have the possibility of eternal life.

The rational or human soul is the first actuality [or Breath of Life that directs an organism toward self-fulfillment] of an elementary natural body [consisting of the four elemental qualities] that potentially possesses life and which the soul uses as its instrument in so far as it acts by rational choice and rational deduction, and in so far as it perceives universals. It is the possibility of understanding and gaining scientific knowledge sets human beings apart from other animals.

It is Avicenna's view that the human rational soul does not die with the death of the body. It is immortal and indestructible. Avicenna concludes his arguments about the immortality of the human soul, saying:

> . . . .the corruption of the body would entail the corruption of the soul only if the body exists co-dependently with it, or it is either a cause or essential effect of the soul. Since none of these types of dependence relations applies to the relation between body and soul, the death of the body need not entail the destruction of the human soul. The [human] soul can and does survive the body's death, continuing to carry on an intellec-

tual existence wholly disassociated from the body, an existence of true blessedness and the afterlife.[39]

Avicenna's famous argument that proves the existence of the human or rational soul/intellect and consciousness is known as that of the flying person where he proves the presence of self-awareness:

> One of us must suppose that he was just created at a stroke, fully developed and perfectly formed but with his vision shrouded from perceiving all external objects—created floating in the air or in space, not buffeted by any perceptible current of the air that supports him, his limbs separated and kept out of contact with one another, so that they do not feel each other. Then let the subject consider whether he would affirm the existence of his self.
>
> There is no doubt that he would affirm his own existence, although not affirming the reality of any of his limbs or inner organs, his bowels, or heart or brain, or any external thing. Indeed he would affirm the existence of this self of his while not affirming that it had any length, breadth or depth. And if it were possible for him in such a state to imagine a hand or any other organ, he would not imagine it to be a part of himself or a conditions of his existence.
>
> But you know that what is affirmed is distinct from what is not affirmed, and what is implied is distinct from what is not implied. Thus the self, whose existence he affirmed, is his distinctive identity, although not identical with his body and his organs, whose existence he did not affirm.
>
> Accordingly, one who directs his thoughts to this consideration has a means of affirming the existence of the soul as something distinct from the body, indeed, as something quite other than the body, something which he knows through his own self-consciousness, even if he had overlooked it and needs to be alerted to it.[40]

Avicenna further elaborates on this:

> Reflect upon your self and consider, if you were in good health, that is of sound intellect, but differently situated than you are, could you be unaware of your own existence? Could you fail to affirm the reality of the self? I do not think that any rational person could deny such a fact. Even if he were asleep or drunk, self-awareness would not be completely absent, even though one would not be consciously representing his own existence continually to himself.
>
> Suppose your being to have been just begun. You are of sound and capable intelligence, but your bodily parts are so disposed that you cannot see them or touch your limbs or organs; they are separated from one an-

other and suspended for the moment in thin air. You would find that you were conscious of nothing but your own reality.

By what means would you be conscious of your self at that moment, or at the moment just before or after it? What would it be in you that had such awareness? Do you find any of your sensory faculties that could play this role? Or would it be your mind, a power quite other than the senses or anything connected to them? If it is your mind, and it is a power distinct from the senses, is its awareness mediated or unmediated?

I don't see how, in this particular moment, you would need anything to mediate your awareness. Rather, your consciousness at this moment is unmediated, and it follows that you can be conscious of your self without reliance upon any other power or the intervention of any other power. . . .Does it occur to you to ask whether the vehicle of your awareness is not the skin that you can see with your own eyes? It is not. Even if you shed your skin and acquired another, you would still be you ...[41]

You might say: 'I affirm my own reality only through awareness of my own actions.' But, if so, you must have some action that you affirm in our illustration, some motion or some other act. But we excluded that, by hypothesis. And even though you speak of an action in the most general terms, this action of yours, if you posit and action categorically, must have a subject categorically. And that precisely is your self.

Self-awareness is further explained as being aware of our essence:

In self-awareness, thinks Avicenna, one consciously reflects on oneself as an object of intellection. As such, self-awareness might be thought of as a second-order awareness: being aware of oneself as an object of awareness. Avicenna, however, also identifies a more basic or primitive form of self-awareness that he believes is essential not only to the intellect but also to the human soul more generally. This primitive self-awareness is the subconscious awareness of the *I* that accompanies all of one's actions and conscious experiences, underlying and unifying them. It is for Avicenna our awareness of the very substance of our soul considered independently of its relation to the body and bodily activities.[42]

Avicenna describes how the the animal soul assists the rational soul/intellect:

We say that the animal powers assist the rational soul [intellect] in various ways, one of them being that sensation brings to the rational intellect particulars from which result four intellectual processes.

First of all, from these particulars the soul abstracts single universals by abstracting their concepts from their matters, material attachments and accidents by considering the common factors and differences, and by distinguishing the essential from the accidental. From this the rational intellect receives the fundamental concepts by using the powers of imagination and estimation.

Secondly, the soul finds relations of negation and affirmation between these separate universals. Where this combination by negation and affirmation is self-evident, it simply accepts it. Where this is not the case, it leaves it till the discovery of the middle term.

Thirdly, it acquires premises verifiable by observation, or experience that consists in finding—through sense-experience—the necessary attribution of a positive or negative predicate to a subject, or in finding a contradictory opposition (i.e., the human being is rational, the human being is not rational; the human being is not a non-rational being), or in finding a consequence of a positive or negative conjunction (i.e., if it is day it is light; if it is not day it is not light); in finding a positive or a negative disjunction without contradictory opposition (i.e., either it is day or it is night; it is neither black nor is it white).

This relation is valid not sometimes nor in half the number of the cases but always, so that the soul acquiesces in the fact that it is of the nature of this predicate to have such-and-such relation to this subject, or that it is of the nature of this consequence to follow necessarily from this antecedent or to be essentially contrary to it—not·by mere chance.

Thus, this would be a belief obtaincd from sense-experience and from reasoning as well: from sense experience, because it is observed; from reasoning, because if it were by chance it would not be found always or even in most cases.

It is just as we judge that scammony is, by its nature, a laxative for bile, for we have experienced this often and then reasoned that if it were not owing to the nature of scammony but only by chance, this would happen only on certain occasions.

In the fourth category are the reports to which the soul gives assent on account of unbroken and overwhelming tradition.

The rational intellect, then, requires the help of the body in order to acquire these principles of conception and judgment. Having acquired them, it returns to itself. If, after that, any of the lower powers happens to occupy it, this completely diverts it from its proper activity. When not so diverted it does not need the lower powers for its special activity, except in certain matters wherein it particularly needs to refer once more to the power of imagination for finding a new principle in addition to what had already been obtained or for recalling an image.

This happens frequently in the beginning, but seldom afterwards. When the soul becomes perfect and strong (i.e. has obtained all the principles it needs for conception and judgement), it isolates itself absolutely in its actions, and the powers of sensation and imagination and all the other bodily powers divert it from its activities.

For example, a man may need a riding animal and other means of reaching a certain place; but when he has reached it and done his work and feels reluctant to leave on account of certain events, the very means which he employed to get there would indirectly prove an impediment.[43]

THE INTELLECT

When the human soul, that is potentially an "intellect", is activated by the Active Intellect, it actualizes the function of cognition and reasoning. The soul is then called "intellect". The intellect differs from the soul in that the soul is the active agent, the first perfection, and the intellect is its instrument like a sword (soul) and its ability to cut (intellect).

THE THEORETICAL INTELLECT

It is through the theoretical intellect that humans reason, think and abstract ideas. Through the intellection and intuition of the creative power of knowledge, the theoretical intellect receives knowledge. It is innately predisposed to manage universal images, images that are completely separate from matter. The function of the theoretical intellect is to abstract intelligibles from matter, space and position. The power to do this has been given by the soul's power of perception. The power of perception, in turn, acts through the human, rational intellect in the world of matter and pure ideas to abstract the intellectual from matter by means of the external and internal senses. The theoretical intellect operates through four levels: material, habitual, actual and acquired intellects. These describe how the learning process works (see below).

THE SPIRITUAL INTELLECT

From the acquired intellect, a secondary process of the theoretical intellect, comes the spiritual intellect that allows human beings to enter the world of intuition and at the highest level, it is the intellect exhibited by prophets.

According to Avicenna, all knowledge comes from the human ability to receive immaterial forms. When the forms are actually physical matter, our degree of knowledge about the thing depends upon our ability to abstract from the physical.

The other way we obtain knowledge is through immaterial forms themselves and this, he says, is the highest form of knowledge. An example

would be that the real nature of a human being, its "whatness" is an immaterial form. However, when this immaterial form becomes part of a physical
form, it only accidently relates to the physical form whereby it becomes:

> . . . .subject to material attachments and relationships such as multi-
> plicity, a definite quantity, quality, place, and position.[44]

If these conditions were part of the "whatness" of being human, all
human beings would be equal in regard to them.

> . . . . the acquired intellect attains to higher forms of intellect graded in
> various degrees of excellence. In relation to the higher planes of existence,
> the acquired intellect is none other than the spiritual intellect that charac-
> terizes the intellects of the prophets, the saints, and the learned who are
> established in knowledge, each according to their various degrees of ex-
> cellence.[45]

Proof of the spiritual intellect is intuition through the Active Intellect.
The Active Intellect's function, as will be explained in the next part, functions in regard to intelligibles as the Giver of Forms does in regard to sensible forms.

> The acquisition of knowledge, whether from someone else or from
> within oneself, is of various degrees. Some people who acquire knowl-
> edge come very near to immediate perception, since their habitual intel-
> lect is the most powerful.
> If a person can acquire knowledge from within himself, this strong
> capacity is called intuition. It is so strong in certain people that they do
> not need great effort, or instruction and actualization, in order to make
> contact with the Active Intellect. But the primary capacity of such a per-
> son for this is so powerful that he might also be said to possess the second
> capacity; indeed, it seems as though he knows everything from within
> himself. This is the highest degree of this capacity. In this state the mate-
> rial intellect must be called Divine Spirit. It belongs to the genus of the
> habitual intellect, but is so lofty that not all people share it. It is not un-
> likely, indeed, that some of these actions attributed to the Divine Spirit
> because of their powerful and lofty nature overflow into the imagination
> which symbolizes them in sense-imagery and words . . . .
> What proves this is the evident fact that the intelligible truths are ac-
> quired only when the middle term of a syllogism is obtained. This may
> be done in two ways: sometimes through intuition, which is an act of
> mind by which the mind itself immediately perceives the middle term.

This power of intuition is quickness of understanding. But sometimes the middle term is acquired through instruction, although even the first principles of instruction are obtained through intuition, since all knowledge can be reduced ultimately to certain intuitive principles handed down by those who first accepted them to their students.[46]

Avicenna speaks of the 'middle term' used in logic. A middle term can be either the subject or predicate of a categorical proposition. It may appear in both the major and minor premise, but not in the conclusion or it may be the middle term. In this case, the middle term has to be in one premise, but not in the conclusion. It is a term that appears as a subject or predicate of a categorical proposition: (1) in both premises but not in the conclusion of a categorical syllogism. (2) The middle term (in bold below) must be distributed in at least one premise but not in the conclusion.

Example:
Major premise: All **men** are mortal.
Minor premise: Socrates is a **man**.
Conclusion: Socrates is mortal.
(The middle term is in bold.)

Avicenna continues:

It is possible that a person may find the truth within himself, and that the syllogism may be effected in his intellect without any teacher. This varies both quantitatively and qualitatively; quantitatively because some people possess a greater number of middle terms which they have discovered themselves; and qualitatively because some people find the term more quickly than others. Now, since these differences are unlimited and always vary in degrees of intensity, and since their lowest point is reached in people who are wholly without intuition, so their highest point must be reached in people who possess intuition regarding all or most problems, or in people who have intuition in the shortest possible time.

Thus there might be a person whose soul has such an intense purity and is so firmly linked to the rational principles that he·blazes with intuition, i.e., with the receptivity of inspiration coming from the Active Intellect concerning everything.[47]

Avicenna next explains the difference between transmitted knowledge and intellectual knowledge. The difference is that of "following authority" or "imitation" (*taqlid*) and "verification" or "realization" (*tahqiq*). These are two basic ways of gaining knowledge. Someone who knows innately knows "the middle term of a syllogism" is someone who, as Avicenna explains, does not accept them merely on authority, but because of their logical order or causes.

> So the forms of all things contained in the Active Intellect are imprinted on his soul either all at once or nearly so, not that he accepts them merely on authority but on account of their logical order which encompasses all the middle terms. For beliefs accepted on authority concerning those things which are known only through their causes possess no rational certainty. This is a kind of prophetic inspiration. Indeed its highest form. It is the highest human power.[48]

It is through this spiritual intellect that Avicenna explains the knowledge that the prophets had.

> Whereas today we tend to think of prophecy, veridical dreams, and the like as outside the scope of scientific inquiry, Avicenna did not. He, like all of those around him, took such events as factual phenomena, and as such they are for him just as open to scientific scrutiny and in need of scientific explanation as any other natural phenomenon. . . . He found such an explanation in psychology. . . .
> The person with insight is, with relative ease, able to make initial contact or conjunction with the Active Intellect, which again brings about intellectual perception. In fact, continues Avicenna, for some people their insight is so intense that it is as if they know everything on their own without being taught those things. Moreover, they recognize these things almost immediately. In these very few individuals with the highest level of insight—which Avicenna identifies with prophets—their insight so abounds that it overflows and deluges their imagination in the form of visions and voices.[49]

THE PRACTICAL INTELLECT

The practical intellect, under the direction of the theoretical intellect, manages the body and motivation.

> In so far as the practical intellect functions as the practical intellect, it is the principle of movement of the human body.
> In relation to the motivational power of the animal soul, which is responsible for the exertion of willing that desire (attraction to pleasure) or aversion (avoidance of harm/pain) shall issue in action, it produces human emotions.

In relation to the perceptive power and its retentive, estimative, and imaginative powers, it manages physical objects and produces human skills and arts; and in relation to its power of rational imagination it gives rise to premises and conclusions. In so far as it governs and manages the human body it induces ethical human behavior involving the recognition of positive and negative traits.[50]

The practical intellect of the soul inclines towards the management of the body in issuing ethical principles and discerning between the positive and negative traits or moral values. It receives its knowledge from the theoretical intellect.

In doing this, the practical intellect or reason governs over two of the motivational powers as its function is of extreme importance to Avicenna's psychology. These two powers are the attraction to pleasure (concupiscent) and avoidance of harm/pain (irascible) or lust and anger, the "passions". The process of how the practical intellect governs and manages these two powers of the soul is described in Part Four as Avicenna's Final Cause.

PART TWO: THE CAUSES OF THE SOUL
CHAPTER 1: THE MATERIAL CAUSE
INTRODUCTION

In regard to cause and response to the question "why?" of the soul, an inquiry is made into nature and its relationship to why the soul exists or comes into existence? Why it goes out of or does not go out of existence?

The best way of understanding the "why" of the soul as part of living bodies is to understand what changes, according to Avicenna. What is the relationship of the soul as perfecting and enlivening the body as matter? What it is that causes the soul to change?

Avicenna answers this through four causes: The Material, the Formal, the Efficient and the Final.

The material cause is the change or movement of the soul determined by the materials being changed. The Material Cause includes the four elements, the four humours, the organs and the temperament. The four elements, four humours, and the organs are considered by Avicenna to be the quantitative pattern of organization or structure of the soul and its changes, while temperament is its qualitative pattern.

Avicenna points out that while there are a multiple of material forms, they become so thoroughly altered and integrated that from an initial multiplicity and diversity, a holistic unity emerges with a specific structure and a specific temperament.[51]

> The elements, water, air, fire and earth,
> Have taken their station below the heavens
> Each serving diligently in its own appointed place,
> Before or behind which it never sets its foot.
> Though all four are contrary in their nature and position,
> Still one may see them ever united together.
> Inimical are they to each other in essence and form,
> Yet united into single bodies by fiat of necessity.
> From them is born the three-fold kingdom of nature.[52]

THE FOUR ELEMENTS

In regard to the elements, Avicenna identifies them as earth, water, air and fire. They each have two elemental qualities: earth is cold and dry; water is cold and wet; air is hot and wet; fire is hot and dry.

In regard to their functions, hot is considered to diffuse and separate; cold draws things together; wetness receives impressions; while dryness preserves them. The elements mix together in various proportions through causes of interaction that include the movements of the heavenly bodies. Through the mixing, they form composite bodies that make up the various orders of things in nature through the various temperaments.

Avicenna states that natural science speaks of four elements and no more. Two of these are light and two heavy. Fire and air are light while earth and water are heavy.

> The four elements out of which all sublunary beings are composed consist basically of the same matter which on different occasions accepts different forms. They are therefore transformed into each continuously. This transformation is accomplished by the rejection of one form and the acceptance of a new one. These changes, however, are not autonomous or independent. They are brought about by the [Active Intellect], that gives order to all activities in the sublunary region and which is also the principle of the [mineral], plant, animal, and the human kingdoms.[53]

In addition, according to Avicenna, each elemental property in the region between the moon and the earth has a natural place, its place being dependent upon its composition of elemental qualities. It is constantly moving because of a yearning to return to that place:

> All motion in this region between the moon and the earth is in fact due to the desire or inclination within things return to the place that corresponds to their nature.[54]

Water, cold and wet, is above Earth, cold and dry. Air, hot and wet, is above water. Fire, hot and dry, is above air.

> Therefore, each of the four elements possess a nature which is its lot and its perfection; fire has one, water another, air another and earth another. And these qualities are accidents that come from that nature and that perfection.[55]

The presence of these elements are causes, for instance, for lightning where there is the sudden burning up of dryness. Heat and dryness almost become free of cold and moisture. Thunder is described as the colliding of heat and dryness in air that becomes unsteady by the winds. The clouds in their heaviness put pressure on the winds because cold, dryness and moisture are inclined toward their own centers.

The function of the elements is to move in a rectilinear form in mutually opposite direction resulting in continuous change that is either cyclical or progressive. Cyclical change relates to physiology while progressive change manifests as growth.

What is important to note in studying Avicenna's psychology and the soul, is not the soul in itself, but the changes that take place instead of matter. Matter exists by virtue of the ceaseless creative power of God. It has no reality apart from his power. Matter would cease to be the moment He withheld his power.

FIRE: HOT AND DRY

Fire is a simple substance whose natural position is above all the other elements. Its dryness permits forms to be assumed only with difficulty and they are resolved with similar difficulty.

AIR: HOT AND MOIST

Air, as with the other elements, is considered by Avicenna to be a simple substance which lies above water and beneath fire. This is because of its relative lightness. Its function is to rarefy and render things finer, lighter, more delicate, softer, and consequently better able to move to the higher spheres.

WATER: COLD AND MOIST

Water is a simple substance which in its natural state surrounds the earth and is, in its turn, surrounded by the air, subject of course, to the other elements being also present in their own natural positions. Its position is based on its relative density.

Water appears to our senses as long as there are no influences to counteract it. It lends itself readily to dispersion and thus assumes any shape without permanency. It allows things to be molded and spread out and attempered in their construction because, quite unlike the earth, it easily parts with its old shape and readily accepts a new one. Being moist, shapes can be readily made with it and as easily lost and resolved.

When dryness and moisture alternate, dryness is overruled by the moisture, and thus the object is easily susceptible to being molded into a form whereas if the moisture were overruled by dryness, the form and features of the body would become firm and constant. Moisture serves to protect dryness from causing something to crumble or break up. Dryness, on the other hand, prevents moisture from dispersing.

EARTH: COLD AND DRY

Earth is a simple substance. In this position it remains stationary, but when away from the center, it tends to return to its normal position. This is the reason for its intrinsic weight. These qualities of the earth can be easily appreciated by our senses as long as there is no interference by extraneous agents and it obeys its particular nature. It is by means of the element of earth that the parts of our body are fixed and held together into a compacted form. This is how our outward form is maintained.

THE FOUR HUMOURS

The humours within the human being are the transformed elements and their elemental qualities in the universe. They profoundly affect the function of the soul's governance of the body.

THE NATURE OF THE HUMOURS

Following the humoural pathology of Hippocrates, Islamic medicine [and psychology] considers the 'elements' [and their elemental qualities of heat, coldness, moisture and dryness] to be . . . . to the body what the four elements [elemental qualities] are to the world of nature. . . .Just as in the world of generation and corruption, everything comes into being from the mixture of the four elements, so in the human body there is a humoural constitution brought into being from the mixture of the four humours that marks the state of health of the body.[56] (S. H Nasr, *SCI*, pp. 219-220)

According to Avicenna, humour or body-fluid is that fluid, moist, physical substance into which our aliment is transformed. That part of the aliment which has the capacity to be transformed into body substance, either by itself or in combination with something else, is capable of assimilation by the members or organs and completely integrated into the tissues. This is the healthy or good humour. It is what replaces the loss which the body substance undergoes.

The residue from this process, or the excess is called unhealthy or abnormal humour. It is the fluid which, in the absence of proper digestion or conversion, is unsuitable for assimilation and is therefore eliminated from the body.

According to Avicenna, the non-excreted fluids have not as yet been subjected to the action of any of the simple members or organs and they are to be changed until they reach the tissues for which they are destined. The fluid which is present in the tissues as dew drops and is capable of being utilized as a nutriment in times of dire necessity, also moisten the organs which have been dried up by excessive activity is known as Radical Moisture (see below).

It should be noted the refinement of the mixture of the humours is what gives the soul its perfection:

> The more refined the mixture of the humours, the greater the perfection and the more complete and perfect the possibility of receiving the soul. Moreover, in each person, health means the harmony of the humours and illness the disruption of the balance of the temperament.
>
> The harmony is never perfect in any person, but relative to his own temperament, health means the re-establishment of the balance of the humours. Diagnosis for such disorders as fever are in fact based on searching for the way in which the balance of the humours has been upset.[57]

THE FOUR HUMOURS

Both the normal and abnormal humours are of the following four varieties: the bilious humour, the sanguineous humour, the most excellent of all, the serous humour, and the atrabilious humour.

THE BILIOUS HUMOUR: HOT AND DRY (FIRE)

According to Avicenna, the bilious humour is the foam of blood. It is bright in color. It is light and pungent. The more red, it is, the hotter it is. It is formed in the liver and then follows one of two courses: either it circulates with the blood or it passes on to the gallbladder. The part which passes into the blood stream functions for two purposes.

First of all, the portion which goes to the blood is essential for nutrition of organs like the lungs. It makes the blood light and thin for easy passage through the narrow channels of the body. The portion which goes into the gallbladder is thus prevented, from spoiling or impairing the body and providing nutrition to the gallbladder. Its subsidiary functions are the cleansing of the intestine from the thick and viscid mucus and stimulation of the musculature of the intestine and rectum for proper defecation.

That is why stasis or obstruction in the bile duct may produce colic.

Besides the normal clear bilious humour in the liver and blood, there are seven abnormal types, of which the first four are so by admixture of an alien substance:

One, *citron-yellow* bile in the liver due to the admixture of unnaturally thin serous humour, less hot than normal bile;

Two, *yolk-like-yellow* bile, the color of egg-yolk in the liver due to admixture of coagulated serous humour, still less hot.

Three, *ruddy-yellow* oxidized bile, an opaque fluid in liver and blood due to simple admixture of atrabilious humour, and somewhat causing harm or damage;

Four, *oxidized* bile of another type in the gall-bladder due to spontaneous oxidation resulting in a thin fluid plus an ash that does not separate out; more harmful or detrimental than the last.

The three abnormal biles that result from internal change of substance are:

Five, *hepatic* bile in the liver due to oxidation of the unnaturally thin part of the blood so that its denser part separates out as atrabilious humour; a moderately toxic bile;

Six, *gastric leek-green* bile in the stomach due to intense oxidation of vitelline bile; less toxic than the last; and

Seven, *mildew* or *verdigris-green* bile in the stomach due to intense oxidation of yolk-like-yellow bile and loss of all its moisture; very hot, and extremely toxic

Of these, Avicenna states, the seventh is possibly derived from the sixth through increased oxidation resulting in total drying out that would account for its whitish hue.[58]

THE SANGUINEOUS HUMOUR: HOT AND MOIST (AIR)

The nature of the sanguineous humour may be normal or abnormal, conforming to its nature or not. Normal blood is red in color, sweet in taste and free from smell.

Abnormal blood has two varieties: first of all, blood which has become abnormal from some intrinsic change in the temperament, such as getting hot or cold, but not because of any admixture with any foreign matter and second of all, blood which has become abnormal from admixture with some morbid or unhealthy fluid derived from within or without.

This second type of abnormal blood may be caused by either an unhealthy fluid coming to it from without, penetrating it and so causing decomposition in it or by a putrescent change in a portion of itself (the rarefied product becoming bilious humour and the denser product becoming atrabilious where either one or both together may remain in the blood).

Abnormal blood of the first type is named according to what which is mixed with it—whether serous humour or atrabilious or simply bilious fluid. Abnormal blood of the second type is named according to its color and wateriness—sometimes it is turbid, sometimes attenuated, sometimes very dark from much blackness, sometimes pale and its taste and bitter, salty or sour.[59]

THE SEROUS HUMOUR: COLD AND MOIST (WATER)

The nature of the serous humour may be normal or abnormal. Normal serous humour can be transformed into blood at any time as it is an imperfectly matured blood. It is a kind of sweet fluid which is only slightly colder than the body, but it is much colder than the bilious and sanguineous humours.

Sweet serous humour has a variety which is abnormal. This variety is tasteless unless it is mixed with blood, when it becomes somewhat sweet. This happens frequently with sputum and catarrhal excretions.

According to Galen, the normal variety of the sweet serous humour has no special place in the body, as is also the case with the bilious and atrabilious humours. The reason is that like blood, the serous humour is required by nearly every organ in the body, hence, it always circulates with the blood.

There are two special reasons why it has no special place. The first reason is essential and the second is accessory.

The essential function is two-fold: the serous humour has necessarily to remain in close contact with the tissues as an easily available material for emergencies, such as a temporary failure of the food supply from the stomach and liver as in starvation. This material is normally acted upon by the vegetative ability or powers or drives which change and digest it and are themselves maintained thereby.

The transformation of lymph into blood is achieved by the Innate Heat (see below). Alien heat [bacterial infection] would only putrefy the material and decompose it. This kind of relationship does not hold in the case of the two bilious fluids because neither of them turns into blood at any time as the serous humour does under the influence of Innate Heat. However, they resemble the serous humour in undergoing putrefaction and decomposition under the influence of alien heat [bacterial infection].

Secondly, the serous humour must be mixed with the sanguineous humour before it can reach and nourish the tissues of the lymphatic temperament. When the serous humour is present in the blood for subserving nutrition, it must be in definite proportion before it reaches the parts to be nourished, that is, the brain. It is the same in the case of the two bilious humours. The accessory function is that of moistening the joints, tissues and organs concerned in movement. Otherwise the heat of the friction of the movement would produce dryness of their surfaces. This function is within the range of necessity.

There are several different types of abnormal serous humour or phlegm:

The *sticky* and of an apparently abnormal consistency; immature, but of an apparently normal consistency; abnormally thin and watery; and thick and of white color. The thinner portions of the serous humour are dispersed by stagnation in the joints and passages. This is the thickest of all varieties.

Another variety of the serous humour is the one which is salty and is more dry than all the other types. The *salty*, serous humour is warmer, drier, and lighter than any of the other types. It is salty because the oxidized earthy matters of dry temperament and bitter taste are mixed with the watery (nearly or quite insipid) moisture in equal [in terms of potency, not weight] proportions. If these particles are in a greater quantity than the normal, the fluid becomes bitter instead of salty. Both natural and artificially manufactured salts are made in this way. With the artificial method, alkaline, ash-like or lime is boiled in the water and then filtered out. The remaining solution is then either boiled to yield a deposit of the dissolved salt or is left to crystallize out.

Unlikely *thin* serous humour may be insipid or have only a slightly salty taste. This taste comes from the mixture with an equal amount of oxidized bile which is dry and bitter. The resultant heating salty fluid is called "bilious serous humour." The taste of salt in the serous humour is due to the oxidized portion of the serous humour that is turned into a sort of dry ash which makes it salty. Mixture with the fluid alone would not give salinity to the serous humour, unless the other factor, (i.e., the oxidized ash) is also present.

The serous humour becomes *bitter* if mixed with the atrabilious humour (which is itself bitter) or too much infrigidation tales place whereby the taste changes from sweet to bitter. The process consists in a congealing and degradation of the watery element into something dry and, therefore, earthy in character. The degree of heat is too little to ferment it and make it sour. A strong heat would completely alter it into something else.

The serous humour, which is *sour*, has also two varieties. One is where the sourness is intrinsic in origin and the other is where it is introduced from without. In the latter case it is acrid atrabilious humour that is the extraneous factor. This will be discussed later. When the sourness is intrinsic, it is comparable with the change that takes place when the others juices go sour. In other words, it is sour because the humour has fermented and then gone sour.

There is a variety of serous humour which is *bitter*. The astringent taste in this humour may be due either to an admixture of some astringent atrabilious or bilious itself may become so cold that it tastes astringent. This is because cold solidifies the moisture into earthy particles and in this process the heat being neither so little as to ferment it into sour serous humour nor so strong as to mature it into an assimilable form makes it astringent.

Serous humour may be *thick* and viscid like melted glass or it may be sour or tasteless. In fact, it should not be surprising if the tasteless variety of the thick serous humour proves to be really an immature humour or if the immature humour turns out to be an altered form of the tasteless kind. This serous humour is originally cold and thin and is free from putrefaction and admixture of any kind. Its greater cold and viscosity are due to its local stagnation. It is now clear that the abnormal serous humour has four varieties in regard to taste: salty, sour, bitter and tasteless. The latter also has four varieties: watery, slimy, viscid and thick white. The immature serous humour is really a variety of the slimy.[60]

THE ATRABILIOUS HUMOUR: COLD AND DRY (EARTH)

Atrabilious humour has a natural and abnormal variety. Normal atrabilious humour is a sediment of the normal blood. It has a taste between sweetness and bitterness. After being formed in the liver, a part goes to the blood and another to the spleen.

The part which goes with the blood functions for two purposes: the nutrition of organs such as the bones which have an appreciable quantity of the atrabilious bile in their composition, and to make the blood properly thick and heavy.

The portion that is in excess of these requirements is taken up by the spleen essentially for its own nutrition but also to save the blood from being damaged. The portion which goes from the spleen into the stomach serves the purpose of making the stomach strong and firm. It also stimulates the appetite by its sour taste.

This action of atrabilious humour is somewhat similar to that of the bilious humour. Just as the surplus of bile in the blood goes to the gallbladder, and the surplus from the gallbladder passes into the intestine, the excess of atrabilious humour from the blood goes to the spleen, what is left over from the spleen goes to the stomach to induce appetite. The surplus of bilious humour excites peristaltic movements and thus assists evacuation, but the surplus of atrabilious humour encourages the intake of food.

According to Avicenna, the abnormal form of atrabilious humour is formed by the oxidation of material or ash formed from an oxidation of the commingled bilious humour. When there is some earthy matter mixed something moist, the earthy matter separates out either by sedimentation, as does normal atrabilious humour, or as an ash by the oxidation process, dispersion of the thinner elements leaving the heavier matter behind. This is what takes place in the humours of which the atrabilious humour is to be excreted is the segregate.

Blood is the only body fluid that yields a precipitate of this kind. Serous humour is too sticky to leave any deposit. It acts like oil. Bilious humour does not do so because it is unusually thin and is deficient in earthy matters. Also, it is constantly moving. Whatever little that is formed is either oxidized or quickly eliminated by the body. Moreover, it can be separated from the blood only in minute traces.

Abnormal atrabilious humour is produced in four types: The ash from oxidized bilious humour is bitter in taste. It differs from the partially oxidized bilious humour in being all ashes, rather than a small quantity of the oxidized bile being still mixed with it. If the ash from the oxidized serous humour is light and thin, its product is salty, otherwise it tastes acid or bitter. The ashes from oxidized sanguineous humour has a sweetly salty taste. If the ash from the oxidation of normal atrabilious humour is thin, its oxidized product is extremely acrid like vinegar. On being spilled, vinegar "boils" immediately, giving a foul acrid smell which even flies shun. When the normal atrabilious humour is thick, its oxidized products are bitter rather than acrimonious.

Three varieties of morbid atrabilious humour are particularly injurious according to Avicenna: (1) oxidized bilious humour where the attenuated portion is removed—there are two types of this kind; (2) sero-atrabilious humour which is less injurious and acts at a slower rate; and (3) choleric-atrabilious humour which is more injurious and undergoes decomposition very readily.

The first atrabilious humour derived from the serous humour is slow in action and not so harmful. The second is more acrid and more injurious but if treatment be begun early, it will be more amenable thereto. A third form effervesces less when poured upon the earth and penetrates the tissues less easily and is more slowly destructive. On the other hand, it is very difficult to disperse or mature or treat by any remedial measures.

Avicenna refutes a theory of Galen's that blood is the only physiological humour and all the others are merely excremental and unnecessary to the body. He says that if blood had been the only nutriment, every organ in the body would have had the same temperament and structure. Bones would not have been harder than the flesh and brain softer than the bones. If the bone is hard, it is because its blood supply contains some hard and black bile material, and if the brain is soft, it is due to soft and moist material in its blood supply.

Moreover, Avicenna says, when blood is withdrawn into a vessel, we see how it shrinks and how its various components visibly separate out: a foam (bilious), a turbid yeast (atrabilious), an albuminous portion (serous) and a watery part such as passes in urine. Some think that physical strength is due to abundance of blood and weakness to is paucity. But it is not so. It is rather this: that the state of the body determines whether a nutriment will benefit it or not.

The other humours can also be actually seen in the blood. Thus, when after the venesection blood is allowed to settle down, it develops a foam on the surface (serous humour or yellow bile). The heavy matter which settles down at the bottom is atrabilious humour (black bile). The material which remains mixed with blood, like the white of an egg, is the serous humour. There is also a watery portion which is mostly excreted in the urine. Water is, however, not of a strictly humoural nature because it is of no nutritional value. Water dilutes the food for its easier passage through the narrower channels of the body. The humours are made of the material which is of a nutritional nature. A thing can be nutritious only if its qualities are similar to those of the body, and a thing which has a qualitative resemblance to the body can only be a compound and not a simple substance like water.

It is not true that the strength of the body depends upon the presence of a large quantity of blood in the body and that weakness is due to its deficiency. Strength or weakness depends upon the amount of nutrition available in the blood and on the quantity actually assimilated by the body.

In Avicenna's view, however, others believe that whether the humours be increased or lessened in amount, the maintenance of health depends on the preservation of a certain quantitative proportion between the several humours, one to another, peculiar to the human body. This is not exactly correct he states. The humours must, besides that, maintain a certain constant quantity. It is not a matter of the composition of one or other humour, but of the body itself. The proportions which they bear one to another must also be preserved.[61]

THE ORGANS
THE HOT ORGANS

There are simple members of the body such as flesh, bones, and nerves. Compound members include the hands and face. These organs are the instruments whereby the passions and actions of the soul are achieved as they act as what Avicenna calls the servants of the soul.

The Breath of Life (*ruh*) and heart, which is the center of vital energy, are hottest in the body. Next is blood which, although produced in the liver, due to its contact with the heart, is hotter than the liver. The next is the liver which is really a mass of almost solidified blood. After this is the flesh which is colder than the liver due to the cold nervous tissue in it. The next is the muscle which due to its cold ligaments and tendons is not as hot as the flesh. After this comes the spleen which, due to its high content of the residue from broken up blood, is not as hot. The kidneys are less hot because they have only a little blood. Then there are the breasts, testicles and muscular coats of the arteries which, in spite of being nervous energy in origin, are warm as they contain hot blood and other vital fluids. The next in order are the veins, which are slightly warmer because of blood in them. Last is skin of the palm, which is evenly balanced.[62]

THE COLD ORGANS

The coldest thing in the body is phlegm. Then in order of coldness are hair, bones, cartilage, ligaments, serous membranes, nerves, spinal cord, brain, solid and liquid fats, and lastly the skin.[63]

THE MOIST ORGANS

Phlegm is the most moist. Next in order are blood, solid and liquid fats, brain, spinal cord, breast, testicles, lungs, liver, spleen, kidneys, muscles and the skin. Avicenna states that this order has been laid down by Galen. He adds that it should be noted that the lungs are not really so moist in structure and temperament as is implied in the list. The primary temperament of an organ is always similar to that of its nutriment, while its secondary temperament is determined by its excrement. The lungs, as Galen himself stated, are nourished by the hot blood which contains an appreciable quantity of the bilious humour. If the lungs are moist it is because of the vapors from below and the catarrhal secretions from above. The liver is more moist than the lungs due to the intrinsic moisture while lungs appear to be moist because of the extrinsic moisture. As they are constantly soaked in the extrinsic moisture (secretions), this makes them even structurally moist in the end. Similar is the case with phlegm and blood. The moisture in the phlegm is of a kind which merely moistens the tissues, while the moisture in the blood is of such a type that it is integrated into the very structure of the organs. Although normally there is more moisture in the phlegm than in the blood, in the maturation of phlegm into blood, it becomes dispersed because normal phlegm is nothing but imperfectly digested blood.[64]

THE DRY ORGANS

Hair is the driest of the tissues. It is, as it were, solid residue from the evaporation of moisture from the ethereal element. Next in order are the bones, which due to dryness, are the hardest of organs. Bones are however, a little more moist than hair, because they are formed from blood and are constantly absorbing moisture from attached muscles so that its fume is dry and it dries up the humours naturally located in bones. This is the reason why they are a source of nutrition for many animals, while hair is reported to be consumed only by bats. Next in order of dryness are cartilage, ligaments, tendons, membranes, arteries, veins, motor nerves, heart, sensory nerves and the skin. Motor nerves are colder and drier at the same time and are therefore in equipoise. The sensory nerves are colder but not drier in proportion and are probably very nearly in equipoise since their coldness is not very far distant from that of the motor nerves.[65]

THE TEMPERAMENT

INTRODUCTION

Temperament is the quality which results from the mutual interaction of the four contrary, primary qualities of elements [heat, coldness, moisture, dryness]. The temperament of each person is singular. No two people can be treated in exactly the same way in anticipation of the same reaction to external stimuli. Each one is unique.

The individual temperaments of each of the organs was actualized when the male sperm and the female ovum united. There are efficient causes that may affect the quality of the individual temperament such as the semen and ovum's temperament, the womb's temperature and quality of the menstrual blood, the latter being the nutriment for the embryo. According to Avicenna, even the qualities of the movement of the heavens at the time of conception may affect the temperament of the embryo.

By dividing up into minute particles, the elemental qualities of the humours in the case of the human soul are able to secure an intimate contact among themselves. These qualities are so minutely intermingled as each to lie in very intimate relationship to one another. Their opposite powers alternately conquer and become conquered until a state of equilibrium is reached which is uniform throughout the whole. It is this outcome that is called the temperament.

Since the primary elemental properties of the humours are four in number (namely: heat, cold, moisture, dryness), it is evident that the temperaments in bodies undergoing generation and destruction accord with these powers.

A simple, rational classification is of two types: (a) Equable or balanced. Here the contrary qualities are present to exactly equal degrees of potency—neither of them being in excess or deficiency. This temperament has a quality which is exactly the mean between the two extremes. (b) Inequable or unbalanced. Here the quality of the temperament is not an exquisitely exact mean between the two contraries, but tends a little more to one than to the other. For example, more hot than to cold; more moist than to dry; or contrariwise.

Avicenna points out that a temperament, as understood by medicine, is never strictly equable or strictly inequable. He says that the practitioner should be aware that the really 'equable' temperament does not actually exist in the human being any more than it exists in any 'member' or 'organ'. Also, the term 'equable,' does not refer to weight but to an equity of distribution. It is this distribution which is the primary consideration—whether one is referring to the body as a whole, or only to some individual organ; and the average measure of the elemental properties in it, as to quantity and quality, is that which standard human nature ought to have—both in best proportion and in equity of distribution. As a matter of fact, the mean between excess and deficiency of qualities, such as is characteristic of the human being, actually is very close to the theoretical ideal.[66]

Disorders within the human being are treated by Avicenna with natural herbs. In regard to the relationship between the temperament of the person being treated and the natural drug being used for treatment, Avicenna has this to say:

> It is worth remembering that when a medicine is referred to as being evenly balanced, it does not mean that its temperament is the same as of a human being, or that it is even similar to it, for it would then be like a human being. It merely means that such a medicine, after being acted upon by the innate heat [metabolized] fails to produce any material change in the normal state of the body, and that its pharmacological actions remain within the limits of normal human temperament. In other words, when this medicine is given to a normal person, it does not produce any appreciable change or imbalance in the body. When it is said that a drug is hot or cold, it does not mean that the physical quality of the drug is particularly hot or cold or that it is colder or hotter than the human body. If this were so there would follow the unwarranted inference mentioned above that an evenly constituted medicine is the one which has exactly the same temperament as the human body. It means just that such a medicine produces a greater amount of heat or cold than what was originally present in the body. A drug which, for example, is cold for the human being may be hot for the scorpion, or the medicine which is hot for the human being may be cold for the serpent. In fact it may also mean that the same medicine may be less hot for one person than for another. This is the reason why physicians are advised to change their medicine when it fails to produce the desired result.[67]

IMBALANCED TEMPERAMENTS

In regard to imbalanced temperaments, it is to discover the nature of one's temperament as well as the tendencies that the temperament has to move away from balance and harmony. This is done through diet, the use of natural herbs, exercise and other factors in order to re-establish the balance and harmony that is equivalent to health.[68]

THE SIMPLE IMBALANCES

The simple imbalance of temperament or intemperaments, according to Avicenna, are where there is an active contrary quality which is in excess. That is the temperament is more hot than it should be, not more moist or drier. This is called hot intemperament. Or the temperament may be more cold than it should be, not more moist or drier. This is known as cold intemperament. Where there is a passive contrary quality which is in excess the temperament may be more dry than it should be, but not more hot nor cold. This is dry intemperament. Or the temperament may be more moist than it should be, but not more hot nor cold. This is called moist intemperament.

Simple imbalances do not last long, he goes on to say, as they tend to be soon converted into compound imbalances. That is, an imbalance in the direction of excessive heat promptly leads to dryness and a change in the direction of cold increases the moisture. Dryness no doubt quickly increases cold in the body, but moisture, if it is excessive, makes it much more cold.

If, however, the increase of moisture is moderately cold, it would appear only after some considerable time. From this it will be clear, Avicenna points out, that heat is generally more favorable than cold for maintaining the proper balance and general health of the body.[69]

THE COMPOUND IMBALANCES

Compound temperaments have a dominance of two qualities: hot and moist, hot and dry, cold and moist, and cold and dry. It is clear that the temperament cannot be simultaneously hotter and colder or drier and moister.

Each one of these imbalances of temperament is further sub-divisible into two forms. First of all, in regard to those apart from any material substance [qualitative, formal], the temperament is altered only in regard to one quality because the fluid pervading it has the same quality as that towards which the body is being changed as a whole. Yet it does not do so unless it be because of heat [in fever] or cold [extraneous cold].

Secondly, in regard to those in which some material substance is concerned, here the body is only affected by the quality of the imbalance because of the increased amount of some particular body-fluid. For instance, the body is cooled by serous humour and heated by leek-green choleric humour.

Imbalance or intemperament in which some material substance is concerned can be of two types: a member may be pervaded by the material substance entering from without or it may be pervaded by the material substance which has reached the tissues of the body and fails to get out through the orifices of the channels or from the cavities of the body. Such retention of material may be the beginning of the formation of an inflammatory mass.[70]

Avicenna then goes on to describe the effects of age, gender and residence on temperament.

CHAPTER 2: THE FORMAL CAUSE

The formal cause is the account of what-the soul-is-to-be.

THE GIVER OF FORMS

Avicenna establishes that the Mover for the actions and activities of a living body is the soul. He calls this Mover, the Giver of Forms (Latin *dator formarum*), an immaterial substance that impresses substantial forms on matter that has been properly prepared, matter being composed of the pure and unmixed elements and acts like a natural force. Its emanations are continuous with a regularity that is similar to nature but they are volitional acts according to Avicenna and, therefore, not the result of a nature.

According to Avicenna, the Giver of Forms is always present and active where there is a material recipient is properly disposed to receive it:

> [As] the Giver of Forms is always producing the forms that make up the various kinds of thing in the sublunar world, then its influence is constant, and there is no explanation of why a given thing that came to be had not previously existed, giving that the Giver of Froms was producing its form even when it was not existing. In short, there has to be [this] other factor . . . to explain its coming to be after not having existed.[71]

It is the Giver of Forms that ensouls the embryo:

> In [Avicenna's] account of the ensouling of an embryo, the (primarily 'chemical') nature of the embryo as it develops makes it suitable to receive its soul—its particular individual soul in the case of a human being at least and this soul emanates from the Active Intellect onto this prepared matter.[72]

The Giver of Forms and its emanation ensouling the body may be compared to radio waves:

> . . . .that are all around us yet not heard, while the preparatory role of natural efficient causes is like tuning a radio. The radio is gradually tuned, but once it is turned to a given station, the radio wave, as it were, instantaneously produces a sound in the radio, which on the present analogy is comparable to a new substance. What is important to note is that most of

the work involved in producing a new substance, in fact, is undertaken by those terrestrial causes that prepare the matter by heating, cooling, drying, and moistening the prior substance, just as most of the work in changing the radio station involves turning the radio's knob.[73]

ACTIVE INTELLECT

Avicenna identifies the Active Intellect with the Giver of Forms in his psychology.

> All evidence suggests that Avicenna saw the Active Intellect and the Giver of Forms as two names for a single entity. Thus, it should not be too surprising that the role that Avicenna assigns to the Giver of Forms in substantial generation has a psychological counterpart in the role of the Active Intellect in intellection [understanding and thinking].[74]

In explaining the Active Intellect, Avicenna compares its relationship to us as that of the sun to the power of vision:

> The relation of the Active Intellect to the soul is like that of the sun to the eye. Without light coming from the sun, the eyes in darkness remain as potential organs of vision; and the objects of sight remain potentially visible. Only when the sun sheds its light do the eyes become actually seeing, and their objects become actual visibles.
> The arrival of the meanings of the particular images whose material attachments have all been abstracted by the illumination of the Active Intellect is due to an immediate apprehension in the soul or intellect caused by the illumination that comes directly from the Active Intellect. The elements of meanings that are in the images are then not the cause of the production of their like in the intellect.[75]

The Active Intellect, we are told by Avicenna, is the formal aspect of the intellect:

> We say that the theoretical intellect in human beings comes into actuality from potentiality through the illumination of a substance whose nature it is to produce light.
> This is because a thing does not come into actuality from potentiality

by itself but through something else which gives it actuality. The actuality which this substance gives to the potential human intellect is the intelligible forms. There exists then something which from its own substance confers and imprints on the soul the intelligible forms. This entity thus has in its essence the intelligible forms, and is therefore essentially an intellect. . . .

This Active Intellect is related to our souls, which are potential intellect, and to the intelligibles, which are potential intelligibles, in the same way as the sun is related to our eyes which are potential percipients, and to the colors which are the potential perceptibles.[76]

The Active Intellect is the lowest of the intellects in the hierarchy of emanations and according to Avicenna, it is identified as the Spirit.

Since the potential intellect cannot by itself become actual, the actualization of the human intellect from absolute potentiality to absolute actuality presupposes the existence of an external intelligence that is always in act and which transforms the human intellect from the state of pure potentiality to that of perfect actuality. This external intelligence is the Active Intellect identified as the Spirit.[77]

The Active Intellect is that which provides the immaterial forms that are free of all matter. In order to do so, it must already have these immaterial forms. If this were not so, the Active Intellect would have held these immaterial forms in potential and not be able to actualize them without another cause.

Avicenna's own novel understanding of many of the key concepts used to explain the Active Intellect, such as his conception of light and vision, make his view uniquely his own.[78]

THE ENERGIES OF THE SPIRIT
THE BREATH OF LIFE

The Breath of Life[79] is the link between the psychic-spiritual and physical worlds. It plays a role in the physiological functions of the soul by preparing it to activate its powers. It is also, as we will see, the Breath of Life that eventually delivers the human or rational soul from the body.

To Avicenna, the beginning of the Breath of Life is as a Divine emanation from potentiality to actuality proceeding without intermission or stint until the form is completed and perfected.

The Breath of Life is first manifested in the heart of the human embryo. According to Avicenna, God created the left side of the heart and made it hollow in order that it should serve both as a storehouse of the Breath of Life and the seat of its creation. He also created the Breath of Life to enable the powers of the soul to be conveyed into the appropriate bodily members. The Breath of Life is the rallying point for the unification of the soul's powers, and a vehicle for the soul's powers to emanate into the various material members and tissues of the body.[80]

BREATH OF LIFE AND THE HUMOURS

The origin of all things, according to Avicenna, is through the Mercy of God. It is this that activates all that is potential until it attains perfection. Just as each of the organs has a specific temperament even though they are created out of the same humours, the difference being in the quantities of humours and their variant qualities, in the same way the energies of the Breath of Life have a specific temperament even though they are also created from the same humours that are essential identical.

The Breath of Life, as previously indicated, was created out of the subtle aspects of the humours and its energies (spirits) as the body was created out of the grosser aspects of the humours and their earthiness. The organs and members of the body are created out of the humours due to the intermingling of the humours in order to attain a single temperament through which the organs are able to accept the soul's life giving powers.

When in a state of potential activity, the vital, natural, nervous energies are referred to as spirits. As they are actualized, they become energies. The Breath of Life activates these three spirits. Each of these three has its own place within the body, function and temperament determined by the mode and proportions of the intermingling of the subtler particles.

This Breath of Life arises in the heart, passes thence into the principal centers of the body as three kinds of energy, lingering in them long enough to enable them to impart to it their respective temperamental properties beginning with the vital energy located in the heart. This is the seat of emotions.

Avicenna states that when the vital energy that enters into the heart is plentiful (as it is when there is plenty of that material from which it is rapidly and constantly being generated); when it is balanced in temperament; when it has a luminous, beautiful and bright substance, then there is a strong tendency to sense well-being.

According to Avicenna, this accounts for the fact that the soul rejoices when it looks towards the light, and is depressed when exposed to darkness. Light is in harmony with the Breath of Life and its vital energy. Darkness is in discord with it.

When the Breath of Life is scanty (as occurs in convalescents, in long-standing illnesses, and in elderly persons); when it is not balanced in character (as in morbid states); and when it is: (a) very dense and coarse in substance (as in melancholy and elderly people), it cannot arouse joy; (b) very delicate in substance (as in convalescents and in women), it will not allow of expansion; and (c) confused (as in melancholy people). In all these cases there is a very strong tendency to depression, sadness and grief.

It is therefore evident that an intense sense of well-being disposes the Breath of Life to well-being, sadness to depression; that associated depressants do not make an impression on one's sense of well-being unless they are vigorous; whereas weak stimulants may and do impress themselves thereon. It is, of course, the other way about in the case of depressants.

The location in the brain of the nervous energy tempers it for receiving the soul's powers of sensation/perception and movement; in the liver as the natural energy for receiving the soul's powers of nutrition and growth; in the generative glands as the natural energy to acquire a temperament which prepares it for receiving the soul's power of reproduction.

Nevertheless, Avicenna explains, the particular recipient requires a specific capacity for reception of the good. A creature cannot receive indifferently. For instance, wool cannot be wool and at the same time have the character of a sword. Water cannot be water and at the same time receive human nature.[81]

THE BREATH OF LIFE AND ENERGIES

According to Avicenna, it is the heart that produces the Breath of Life within the body. The Breath of Life then, through combustion, is transformed into the various other energies (spirits) by the powers of the main organs. The Breath of Life is the energy which the organs receive before they can acquire the capacity for the powers of the soul of sensation/perception and movement and so forth, and for accomplishing the various functions of life. Closely related to the vital energy is that of the emotions of joy and anger because they coincide with the expansion and contraction of the Breath of Life.

It is clear that there is something else preparing the organs for these energies and powers, something akin in temperament to itself—and this something is Breath of Life. This is that Spirit which appears in the Breath of Life at the very moment at which the Breath of Life develops out of the rarefied particles of the humours. Not that the activities of these energies are directly derived from the Breath of Life. It is when the particular portion of the Breath of Life reaches the appropriate parts of the brain that it becomes impressed with the temperament of the brain and thereby becomes adapted for the operations of the soul's powers proceeding from and reposing in it. The same applies in the case of the heart, liver and reproductive organs.[82]

THE VITAL ENERGY

The Breath of Life first infuses into the heart where it undergoes combustion as it mixes with the blood and becomes the Breath of Life that actualizes the vital energy (located in the heart and associated with arterial blood). The heart serves as the center of the production of the light and vapory parts of the humours.

The function of the Breath of Life in the heart is to activate the vital energy circulating in the blood and metabolizing the smallest living organisms or the cells. The vital energy is hot and dry. Its center is in the left ventricle of the heart. It preserves life, causes the body to grow, move and reproduce. It travels through the arteries.

THE NATURAL ENERGY

The Breath of Life infuses the natural energy into the liver where it then activates the soul's powers in the humours once the humours have been generated. The natural energy differentiates as it infuses into the four humours, animating their nutritional functions. The sanguineous humour is infused with the power of attraction; the bilious humour with digestion; the atrabilious humour with retention; and the serous humour with expulsion. The natural power (located in the liver and associated with venous blood) is hot and moist. It relates to nourishment, growth and reproduction.

The natural power is of two kinds: (1) One is concerned with the preservation of the individual (irascible) and is responsible for his nutrition and growth. This is located in the liver and its functions emerge from there.

(2) The other is the reproductive power that pertains to the generation and preservation of the species (concupiscent) and is responsible for sexual functions like the formation of germinal fluid and its fertilization of the ovum into the specific form ordained by the Almighty Creator. This power is located in the generative organs. It is in the generative glands that the Breath of Life acquires a temperament that enables it to respond to reproduction. Its functions proceed from them.[83]

THE NERVOUS ENERGY

The Breath of Life infuses nervous energy in the brain activating the soul's powers. The nervous energy is cold and moist. It travels through the nerves. The nervous energy is the closest to the soul in its nature. Coldest in temperament, it has a more subtle heat and is the source for sensation/perception, thought, reason, cognition and motivation and response to stimuli.

When in the brain, it receives a temperament that allows it to respond to the impulses from nerve fibers of sensation/perception, motivation and cognition.[84]

INNATE HEAT

Innate Heat has six functions: (1) It is a product of the Breath of Life; (2) it is first combusted in the heart along with the Breath of Life. There it takes on its form as Innate Heat. This Innate Heat is the basic body heat emitted by all the organs and tissues as a result of the metabolizing of the smallest living organisms or the cells; (3) it is carried with the Breath of Life by the blood to all organs and tissues in order to activate the metabolism of the cells; (4) Innate Heat in the liver is turned into metabolic heat which powers digestion in the natural power. Along with Breath of Life, Innate Heat generates the four humours. Innate Heat "cooks" the humours through a digestive process while the natural power empowers the functions of the humours; (5) Innate Heat in the brain is converted into nervous energy or heat that energizes a type of what can be called mental digestion through the processing of thoughts, ideas and experiences; (6) in the generative or reproductive energy, Innate Heat brings new life.

From middle age on, Innate Heat begins to decline. This is due to the dispersive effect of the atmospheric air on the moisture which is the basic material for heat. The Innate Heat gradually disperses the body's moisture, and the various secretions of the body, are also constantly drying up from normal physical and emotional activity.

RADICAL MOISTURE

Radical Moisture, the material for growth and the matter, according to Avicenna cannot be altered or grown without an efficient cause, as explained in the next chapter. In this case, efficient cause is nature which, according to the will of Almighty God, operates through the Innate Heat.

Avicenna describes four types of secondary body fluids, the primary being the humours. Secondary fluids of the body are either non-excrements or excrements. The non-excrements have not yet been subjected to any action by any of the simple organs and they are not changed until they reach the destined tissues. They are of four types: (1) that which is located at the orifices of the minutest channels near the tissues and thus irrigating them (Latin *cambium*, that is, vascular *cambium* forms tissues that carry water and nutrients throughout the body); (2) that which permeates the tissues like a dew and is capable of being transformed into nutriment if it becomes necessary (Latin *ros*); (3) the third type forms a nutrient which will be changed into the substance of the tissues, whether to the extent of entering into their temperament or to the extent of changing into their very essence, thereby attaining an entire likeness to the member or organ (Latin *gluten*, a grayish, sticky component); (4) the fourth type accounts for the continuous identity of the member or organ or of the body throughout one's life (Radical Moisture, Latin *humidum radicali*). It is derived from the semen, which in its turn is derived from the humours.

INTERACTION BETWEEN INNATE HEAT AND RADICAL MOISTURE

According to Avicenna, the human being takes its origin from two things: (1) the male semen, which plays the part of form; and (2) the female semen (ovum), which provides the matter. Each of these is fluid and moist, but there is more wateriness and earthly substance in the female blood and female sperm, whereas air and fire are predominant in the male sperm.

He remarks that is essential that at the outset of the congelation of the two components there should be Radical Moisture, even though earth and fire are found in the product. The earth provides the firmness and rigidity; the fire provides the maturative power. These give the coagulum (*He cre-*

ated the human being from a clot, Q96:2) a certain hardness or firmness.

Our bodies are exposed to harm from two directions—each having an external and internal cause: the dispersion of Radical Moisture from which we have been created which takes place gradually. The second source is the breakdown causing decay and transformation of the Radical Moisture into a form such that life is no longer able to proceed.

The second source of harm differs from the first in that dryness is here introduced by virtue of depravity of humour; and this dryness continues neutralizing the Radical Moisture of the body until the form ceases to have a capacity for life. Finally, the breakdown through decay disperses the vitality, because it first destroys the Radical Moisture and then disperses it, and simply dry ash is left behind.

Therefore it is clear that these two sources of harm [of the living product of conception] are different from those arising from other causes—such as, freezing cold, torrid heat, grave forms of loss of continuity, various maladies. But it is in regard to the first two named sources of harm that we find the more important factors relative to the question of the preservation of the health [of the soul].

Each of them takes its origin from extrinsic and intrinsic agents. The extrinsic agents are for example, the atmosphere, which is a solvent and decay-causing. The intrinsic agents are, for example, Innate Heat, which is the agent within us through which Radical Moisture is dispersed: the extraneous heat generated within us from nutrients and food, and through other agents which cause decaying changes in the [natural] Radical Moisture.

All these agents mutually aid one another in rendering the body dry. And yet it is true that our perfection and soundness and the power to perform our various actions depend on a degree of dryness of the blood. But the degree of dryness becomes relatively greater and greater until we die. Therefore, this dryness is inevitable.

If we were at the outset essentially composed of Radical Moisture, heat would have to overcome it or else the heat would be choked by it. Therefore the heat continues to exert its own effect, that is, it produces more and more dryness. But whatever degree of dryness there might be at the outset of life, it reaches equilibrium, and remains so until the limit of equilibrium in regard to dryness is reached. The heat remaining constant, the dryness is now relatively greater than before for the matter is less, and hence holds more.

Therefore it is not difficult to understand that the dryness passes on beyond the stage of equilibrium and goes on steadily increasing until the whole of the Radical Moisture of the body is consumed. Therefore, Avicenna says that the Innate Heat is the cause of its own extinction, for it is itself the reason for its own matter being consumed.

Radical Moisture, then, must come to an end and the Innate Heat become extinguished. This occurs sooner if another contributory factor to destruction is present like the extraneous excess of humour arising out of imperfect digestion of food. This extinguishes the Innate Heat by smothering it, enclosing it and by providing the contrary quality. This extraneous humour is called the cold, serous humour. That is how natural or physiological death ensues. The duration of life depends on the original temperament which retains a certain degree of power to the end by fostering its Radical Moisture. (Death from accident or illness has, however, a different origin. Whether from physiological or pathological cause, it is, of course, ultimately determined in accordance with Divine Decree).

Avicenna compares Radical Moisture to the flame of a lamp; the light goes out when all the matter has been used up. As the dryness increases, the Innate Heat diminishes. The loss continues unceasingly till death, and the Radical Moisture which is lost is not restored. The loss goes on more and more.

The dryness (of the body) is increased in two ways: by lessening of the ability to receive matter; by lessening of the Radical Moisture resulting from dispersal of the Innate Heat. The heat becomes more feeble because dryness predominates in the substance of the members, and because the Radical Moisture becomes relatively less.

Avicenna compares the Radical Moisture to the Innate Heat as the oil of a lamp is to the flame. For there are two forms of Radical Moisture in the flame: water, which holds its own, and oil, which is used up. So, in a corresponding manner, the Innate Heat holds its own in respect of the Radical Moisture, but is used up on equal footing with the increase of extraneous heat, due, for example, to defective digestion, which is comparable with the Radical Moisture of the flame. As the dryness increases, the Innate Heat lessens, and the result is natural death.

The reason why the human body does not live any longer than it does lies in the fact that the initial Radical Moisture holds out against being dispersed both by the alien heat and by the heat in the body itself (both that which is innate and that derived from bodily movement). And this resistance is maintained as long as the one is weaker than the other and as long as something is provided to replace that which has been thus dispersed, to wit, from the nutriment or food. Furthermore, as we have already stated, the power or drive which operates upon the food and sustenance in order to render it useful in this way only does so up to the end of life.

Therefore, Avicenna says that the art of maintaining health is not the art of averting death or of averting extraneous injuries from the body or of securing the utmost longevity possible to the human being. It is concerned with two other things: (1) the prevention of breakdown from decay; and (2) the safeguarding of Radical Moisture from too rapid dissipation and maintaining it at such a degree of strength that the original type of constitution peculiar to the person shall not change even up to the last moment of life.

He asserts that this is secured by a suitable diet, namely: (a) one which will ensure the replacement of the Innate Heat and Radical Moisture which are dispersed from the body as exactly as possible; and (b) a diet which will prevent any agents which would lead to a rapid drying from gaining the upper hand excluding agents which produce a normal dryness; (c) one which safeguards the body from the development of decay-causing processes within it and from the influence of alien heat (whether extraneous or intrinsic) because all bodies have not the same degree of Radical Moisture and Innate Heat. There is a great diversity in regard to them.

Moreover, every person has his own term of life, during which the drying up process is inevitable to his temperament and the degree of Innate Heat, and of Radical Moisture can be withstood.

Nevertheless, he points out, factors may arise which assist drying up, or are injurious in some other way. For which reason, many assert that the former are natural causes of death, whereas the latter are accidental. And under this view, the art of maintaining health consists in guiding the body to its natural span of life by paying attention to whatever things conduce thereto.

There are two drives to be fostered by the practitioner in striving for this object as indicated by Avicenna: (1) the nutritive drive whereby that is replaced which is constantly being lost to the body, namely earthiness and Radical Moisture; and (2) the sensitive animal power that is concerned with the replacement of that which is lost to the body by the vital energy namely air and fire. And since food and sustenance are only potentially like the thing nourished, an alternative drive had to be created so that they could be changed actually into the likeness of the thing nourished. In this way the food becomes effective.

The instruments and channels necessary for this had to be created also—namely the means by which material is attracted, expelled, retained, and digested (sequence by sequence, turn by turn).

Therefore, he says that the essential considerations in the art of preserving the health consist in maintaining balance, equilibrium between all these various occurring factors. But there are seven matters concerning which special care must be expended to ensure just proportion: (1) balance of temperament; (2) selection of the articles of food and drink; (3) evacuation of effete matters; (4) safeguarding the composite; (5) maintaining the purity of the air respired; (6) guarding against extraneous contingencies; and (7) moderation in regard to the movements of the body and the motions of the mind, with which may be included sleep and wakefulness.

From all these considerations, Avicenna states that one will now perceive that there is no single fixed limit to which balance or health is to be assigned. Health and balance vary (in range) from time to time. That is to say, it is a state comprised within two limits.[86]

THE POWERS OF THE SOUL

Each of the soul's powers act differently because they perform different functions through different organs at different times. Avicenna even asserts that the powers of the soul are the soul itself.

The soul has in its possession powers that are manifested in bodies according to the nature of the body and the various species including the mineral, the plant, the animal and the human being.

THE MINERAL SOUL'S POWER

The power of the mineral soul is to preserve shape or form.

THE PLANT SOUL'S POWERS

Avicenna begins describing the three powers of the plant soul:

First, the nutritive power which transforms another body into a body similar to that in which it is itself present, and replaces what has been dissolved.

Secondly, the power for growth which increases every aspect of the body in which it resides by length, breadth and depth in proportion to the quantity necessary to make it attain its perfection in growth.

Thirdly, the reproductive power that takes from the body in which it resides a part that is potentially similar to it and acts upon it with the help of other similar bodies, generating and mixing them so as to render that part actually similar to the body (to which it had been only potentially similar).[87]

NUTRITION

According to Avicenna, is not the nutritive power that prepares a member for receiving sensation and motion. It is not the nutritive power that is fundamental for the life of an organ. One cannot say that an organ perishes as soon as the nutritive power is gone. For sometimes the nutritive power ceases in a member and still the member continues to live. Sometimes the nutritive power is unimpaired and nevertheless the member tends towards death.

Nutrition consists of three special functions: (1) Absorption or apposition of the altered material, namely, the blood or a humour which is potentially like the tissue to be nourished. If this process is defective, as may happen in illness, there is 'atrophy', which is a defect of nutrition. (2) Assimilation or agglutination—a later stage. Here the nutriment apposed to the tissue is now fully united up to it and made a part of it. This may be lacking owing to illness and then what happens is called 'fleshy dropsy'. (3) Formation or true assimilation—a stage still further where that which has been made into a part of a member becomes absolutely like it in all respects, in essence and color.

That is, the formative process, though essentially the same throughout the organism, acts differently than organs of the body according to the requirements of their special structures and appearances. Thus, every organ has its own natural power according to its temperament which enables it to acquire its own distinctive color and pattern by making suitable changes in its nutritive material.

Nutrition alters the food in such a way that it becomes temperamentally akin to the body, and is thus rendered suitable for the repair of daily wear and tear of the tissues. The power of growth develops the organs in their appropriate spatial relationships and integrates the nutritive material according to the requirements of the individual growth. Nutrition serves the natural power of growth by providing the necessary nutriment. Sometimes the quantity of nutriment may be sufficient only for the day to day needs of repair, but at times it may be more or less than the daily requirements.

With the plant soul, the real secondary powers are the various processes which assist nutrition which are fourfold: attraction, retention, digestion [ferment actions of the body], and evacuation.[88]

SECONDARY POWERS ASSISTING NUTRITION
ATTRACTION

Aided by the sanguineous humour, the soul's nutritive power assisted by its secondary power of attraction has a quite short duration of muscular contraction and a marked amount of longitudinal movement achieved; the retentive power has a long, continued duration of muscular contraction and a moderate amount of longitudinal movement achieved; the digestive power has a continued duration of muscular contraction and no amount of longitudinal movement achieved; the expulsive power has a momentary duration of muscular contraction and a considerable, but super added from without, amount of longitudinal movement achieved. Therefore the various powers make use of these four qualities in diverse ways and to different extents.

According to Avicenna, the attractive power needs more heat than dryness because the main feature of attraction is movement and movement needs heat. The organs concerned must move rather than be at rest and contracted which requires dryness. This power, however, does not require much movement although at times violent activity becomes necessary. (1) Attraction is brought about by an attractive power—as when a magnet attracts iron; (2) by heat as when oil is drawn up in a lamp. Heat increases the power of attraction exerted by the attractive power.[89]

RETENTION

The soul's nutritive power is aided by the atrabilious humour and secondary power of retention. Retention retains the food while the digestive power is engaged in preparing sound nutritive substances from it. It generally acts through the oblique, but sometimes also through the transverse fibers.

If one compares the degree of active [heat, cold] and passive [dry, wet] quality needed for the various powers, one finds that the retentive power needs more dryness than heat. This is because more time is required for a movement to come to rest than is needed to start the transverse fibers to move in contraction.

Heat is necessary for movement and it takes only a short time to produce its effect so that the remainder of the time is occupied in holding the material and coming to a state of rest. This explains why the temperament of children tends to moistness for their digestive power is weaker.

DIGESTION

The digestive process, aided by the bilious humour, is that which alters the material attracted and held by the soul's attractive and retentive secondary powers. It transmutes the material from its former state until it works up into a temperament such as enables it to become efficient nutrient material. This process is 'digestion' in the strict sense.

At the same time, it produces a change in the superfluities so that they can be easily discharged from the organ containing them. This process is called 'maturation', that is, the liquefaction of the waste products for proper evacuation.

Through it three things happen according to Avicenna: (1) the texture of the superfluities becomes attenuated when it is thickening that hinders expulsion; (2) the texture of the superfluities becomes thickened when it is attenuation that prevents their discharge; (3) the superfluities are entirely broken up if it be viscidity that hinders expulsion. It is a mistake to use the terms 'digestion' and 'maturation' as synonymous.

The digestive power requires more heat than the other three. It does not need dryness but moisture for by moisture the nutrients are rendered fluid and so become able to enter the pores and become molded into the conformation of the channels to be traversed. But one must not suppose that because moisture aids digestion, children (whose temperament is moist) can digest hard or indigestible foods. This can be done in youth, but here the reason is not to be found in their moisture. It is because at that period of life, their nature is similar to that of the foods in question.

Foods of a hard nature are not appropriate for the temperament of children (which is soft) and therefore their transformative power cannot cope with such food. Their retentive power cannot hold it and their expulsive power rapidly expels it. In the case of young people, on the other hand, such hard food is quite suitable for nourishment.

EVACUATION

The evacuation process, aided by the serous humour, is concerned with the evacuation of the non-nutritive excremental matters left over from the digestion of food, the nutritive material taken in excess of nutritional requirements and the material which, having served its purpose, is no longer required like water which is eliminated in the urine.

The waste matter, Avicenna states, is expelled through the natural channels of excretion, that is, the urinary tract for the excretion of urine and large intestine for the evacuation of feces. When, however, these routes are not available, waste matter is diverted either from a superior to an inferior organ or from a hard organ to a soft one. The principle of nature is that when excrements are tending to eliminate through the normal channels, the system helps rather than hinders their evacuation, that is, black bile is eliminated through vomiting.

SUMMARY

According to Avicenna, the real secondary powers of the plant soul are the various processes which assist nutrition which are fourfold: attraction, retention, digestion [ferment actions of the body] and evacuation and their subsidiary qualities of heat, coldness, dryness and moisture.

The action of cold serves all four secondary powers but only indirectly except in so far as it is the contrary of all the powers. All the powers act by virtue of movement which is shown not only as attraction and avoidance or expulsion, but even in the digestion proper process; for the latter consists in the separation of gross and aggregated particles from one another, and in the condensation together of the finer and separated particles.

Cold helps expulsion by: (1) increasing the density of gases; (2) by keeping the particles of the digested material as coarse; (3) and by its astringent action upon the transverse muscular fibers. This action being preparatory, may be regarded as an indirect help. In short, Avicenna remarks, cold helps the powers indirectly, adding that if cold had been concerned directly, there would have been no movement at all and the real purpose would have been completely defeated.

The movements of digestion are simultaneous. Coldness enfeebles, stupefies, and mortifies and hinders this power in all its functions; yet indirectly it helps it by fixing the fibers in the position referred to. Therefore coldness is not directly concerned with the powers. It simply causes their instruments to be in a state which will help to maintain their functions.

The expulsive process requires less dryness than the attractive and retentive process because there is not the need of the muscular contraction requisite for retention nor for the apposition necessary for attraction nor a need to maintain contraction upon an object until the next stage of the process is reached. Nor is there a need for rest, but, on the contrary, there is a need of movement and also a small amount of thickening, just enough to insure that degree of compression and expulsion which is necessary to make the contracted viscous an instrument. Lastly, whereas the retentive power requires a long period of time and the attractive power only a short period—namely that necessary to bring one thing in contact with another—so there is less need of dryness.

The action of dryness is directly instrumental in the functions of two powers—digestion and retention. It is secondary and auxiliary in the case of the other two—attraction and expulsion. This is because dryness delays the movement of the Breath of Life enabling it to take on with it those powers that it has encountered with a vehement impact. It also prevents the moisture present in the substance of the Breath of Life or its instrument from flowing away.

Dryness helps the retentive power because it favors muscular contraction (that is, upon the contents of the organ). The digestive power needs moisture (and not dryness). The action of moisture, on the other hand, hinders strong and free movement by unduly relaxing the fibers. Dryness serves the retentive process by increasing the contractility of the fibers. This is, however, of little use to digestion.

GROWTH

According to Avicenna, growth is possible only when the quantity of nutriment is in excess of the actual requirements. But this would not always produce growth. Thus, after the completion of normal growth, there may be increase of weight, that is, after the recovery from some wasting illness, but this would not constitute growth. Growth is an increase of size within the limits of the normal physical proportions and it can only occur before the completion of full development. Similarly, during the period of growth there may be loss of weight but no reduction in the dimensions of the body, unless of course, this be the result of some special illness.

REPRODUCTION

The reproductive power gives the matter the perfection of the thing; it separates from the parent body a part in which a power derived from its origin inheres and which, when the matter and the place which are prepared to receive its activity are present, performs its functions. It will be evident from the foregoing that all vegetable, animal, and human functions are due to powers over and above bodily functions, and even over and above the nature of the mixture itself.[90]

THE ANIMAL SOUL'S POWERS
MOTION/MOTIVATION

The soul initiates involuntary actions such as initiating and communicating our body. It also serves as the center of motivation.

The soul's power of motivation arouses an action at the same time that it itself is active or an actuator. As the arouser, it creates impulses whereby the impulse directs our moving towards what our soul imagines to be beneficial or harmful. When it imagines something to be beneficial, it arouses its active power to obtain it. When it imagines something to be harmful, it arouses its active power to avoid it or, if the case be, to overcome it.

The soul motivates our will by directing two sub-powers as Avicenna explains: the power of concupiscence (lust, attraction to pleasure) and the irascible power (anger, avoidance of harm/pain):

> The power for motivation again is of two kinds: either it motivates in so far as it gives an impulse, or in so far it causes movement. Now the motivational power, in so far as it provides the impulse, is of two parts: the concupiscent power of lust [attraction to pleasure, preservation of the species] or the irascible power of anger [avoidance of harm/pain, preservation of the individual]. When either a desirable or repugnant image is imprinted on the imagination, it rouses this power to movement.[91]

CONCUPISCENT POWER

> The power of lust or desire (concupiscible, attraction to pleasure) provokes a movement (of the organs) that brings one near to things imagined to be necessary or useful in the search for pleasure.[92]

The generative power or drive is twofold: (1) reproductive—this serves the species and is responsible for the formation of male and female sperm (ovum); (2) the formative power (that is, the male element), which separates from one another the various powers in the sperm and rearranges them in such a way that each organ and tissue receives the temperament appropriate to it. That is, to the nerve, its distinctive temperament and to the bone, its distinctive temperament. The one sperm, apparently homogeneous, opens out in all these directions. This is called the primary transformative power.

Inherent in the informative or plastic power in the female element is the plastic process which, as ordained by the beloved and exalted Creator, gives shape and appearance to the various organs and develops them complete with cavities and holes through which the cranial nerves, arteries, veins and other structures pass in their appropriate spatial relationships and also produces the proper degree of smoothness, roughness, etc.[93]

IRASCIBILE POWER

> The irascible power of anger (avoidance of harm/pain) impels the subject to a movement of the limbs in order to repulse things imagined to be harmful or destructive, and thus to overcome them.[94]

As the source for the power of self-preservation, the soul's power to avoid harm/pain is the location of the healing power of nature:

> The body [and soul] also has the power to preserve and restore that balance that marks the state of health—the power of self-preservation being traditionally called the healing power of nature (*vis medicatrix naturae*).[95]

According to Hippocrates, organisms can often heal themselves. That is, an organism itself does not remain passive to a disorder, but re-establishes balance in counteracting a disorder.

With this view, it is not that one has a disorder, but that one's balance has been disturbed. It is not that a living matter remains passive to an imbalance in the way that non-living matter does. It is in this sense that nature itself is considered to be the "healer of illness".

SENSATION/PERCEPTION

According to Avicenna,

> The perceptive power can be divided into two parts, the external senses and the internal senses. The external senses are five.[96]

THE FIVE EXTERNAL SENSES

Avicenna begins with sight, then hearing, smelling, tasting and touching. These five powers of the soul function to perceive particulars in the outside world.

All sensible forms reach the organs of sense and are imprinted on them, and then the ability or power of sensation perceives them. This is almost evident in touch, taste, smell and hearing. . . .[97]

THE POWER OF SEEING

One of them is sight, which is a ability or power located in the concave nerve; it perceives the image of the forms of colored bodies imprinted on the vitreous humour. These forms are transmitted through actually transparent media to polished surfaces.[98]

THE POWER OF HEARING

The second is the sense of hearing, which is a power located in the nerves distributed over the surface of the ear-hole; it perceives the form of what is transmitted to it by the vibration of the air which is compressed between two objects, one striking and the other being struck—the latter offering it resistance so as to set up vibrations in the air which produce the sound. This vibration of the air outside reaches the air which lies motionless and compressed in the cavity of the ear, moving it in a way similar to that in which it is itself moved. Its waves touch that nerve, and so it is heard. [99]

THE POWER OF SMELLING

The third sense is that of smell, a power located in the two protuberances of the front part of the brain which resemble the two nipples of the breasts. It perceives the odor conveyed to it by inhaled air, which is either mixed with the vapor in the air or is imprinted on it through qualitative change in the air produced by an odorous body.[100]

THE POWER OF TASTING

The fourth sense is that of taste, a power located in the nerves distributed over the tongue, which perceives the taste dissolved from bodies touching it and mingling with the saliva it contains, thus producing a qualitative change in the tongue itself.[101]

THE POWER OF TOUCHING

The fifth sense is that of touch, which is a power distributed over the entire skin and flesh of the body. The nerves perceive what touches them and are affected when it is opposed to them in quality, and changes are then wrought in their constitution or structure.

Probably this power is not one species but a genus including four powers that are all distributed throughout the skin. The first of them judges the opposition between hot and cold; the second that between dry and moist; the third that between hard and soft; and the fourth that between rough and smooth. But their coexistence. in the same organ gives the impression that they are essentially one.[102]

In *The Canon*, Avicenna further elaborates on the sense of touch saying that the sensation of touch is sub-divided into four (pain, temperature, smoothness or roughness, softness or hardness) even though these may all be perceived from by common sense, that is, taste and touch from the tongue and touch and vision from the eyes.[103]

THE FIVE INTERNAL SENSES

There are also five internal senses that internally perceive sensual images and their meanings. They combine or separate them, "conceive notions of them, preserve the conceptions thus conceived, and perform intellection of them."[104]

Avicenna speaks further about the five internal senses:

There are some powers of internal perception which perceive the form of the sensed things, and others which perceive the intention thereof. Some powers, again, can both perceive and act while others only perceive and do not act. Some possess primary perception, others secondary perception.

The distinction between primary and secondary perception is that in the former the percipient power somehow directly acquires the visible form, while in the latter the visible form is acquired through another agent which transmits it to the percipient power.

The distinction between the perception of the physical form and that of the intention is that the physical form is what is perceived both by the inner soul and the external sense; but the external sense perceives it first and then transmits it to the soul, as, for example, when the sheep perceives the form of the wolf, i.e. its shape, form, and color. This form is certainly perceived by the inner soul of the sheep, but it is first perceived by its external sense.

As for the intention, it is a thing which the soul perceives from the sensed object without its previously having been perceived by the external sense, just as the sheep perceives the intention of harm in the wolf, which causes it to fear the wolf and to flee from it, without harm having been perceived at all by the external sense. Now what is first perceived by the sense and then by the internal ability or powers is the form, while what only the internal ability or powers perceive without the external sense is the intention.

The distinction between perception accompanied or unaccompanied by action is this: it is the function of certain internal ability or powers to combine certain perceived forms and intentions with others and to separate some of them from others, so that they perceive and also act on what they have perceived. Perception unaccompanied by action takes place when the form or the intention is merely imprinted on the sense organ without the percipient having any power to act upon it at all.[105]

There are three kinds of perceptive powers of the internal senses.

Some perceive but do not retain their objects; some retain objects but do not act upon them; some perceive their objects and act upon them. Perception is either of the form or the meaning (i.e. the intention or denotation) of the sensible objects; and the senses that retain their objects either retain their forms or their meanings; and those that act upon their objects act upon their forms or their meanings.

The perceiver sometimes perceives directly and sometimes indirectly through another perceptive power. The difference between the sensible form and the meaning is that the sensible form is what is first perceived by the external sense, and then by the internal sense; the meaning is what the internal sense perceives of the sensed object without its having been previously perceived by the external sense.

In the act of perception, the perceiver perceives the form of the external object, that is, an image or representation of the external reality, and not the reality itself. What is perceived by the senses is then not the external reality, but its like as represented in the senses. The external reality is that from which the senses abstract its form.

Similarly, with regard to the meaning, the intelligible forms are representations of realities that are imprinted upon the soul, because the intellect has already abstracted them from the accidental attachments that are foreign to their natures, such as quantity, quality, space, and position.[106]

There are five powers that make up the internal senses: common sense, retaining forms, estimation, memory and imagination. Avicenna divides this into two parts: sensitive imagination and rational imagination. This is the place where the animal soul's powers end while the human rational powers continues.

These powers develop in different degrees. They are not present in their totality in all species of the animal kingdom. By virtue of these powers added to those of the plant and mineral kingdoms, animals are able to perform the various biological functions that belong to their nature. They constitute a degree in the scale of being between the plant world and the human being, and through their physical and psychic qualities form a bridge between the human being and the rest of the terrestrial environment.

The three kingdoms on earth that lead in an ascending order to the human being all consist of the same four elements that act as the ground or substance of manifestation and of the powers of the soul that manifests a different power at each level of existence. The union of a particular power of the soul to a combination of the elements is not as a compound but *ad extra* and by way of a connection. It is brought about when the correct proportion of the elements, reaching a new degree of perfection and approaching closer to perfect equilibrium and harmony attracts to itself a power of the soul.

THE POWER OF COMMON SENSE

Avicenna describes the five internal senses beginning with common sense where the objects of external senses are gathered. The external senses of seeing, hearing, smelling, tasting, touching are only able to grasp one particular type of sensation. It is the internal sense of common sense that grasps all external sensations at the same time. For instance, if sight sees honey, common sense grasps that its color, texture and smell.

The first of the internal senses receives information provided by the external senses. It then combines and separates the internal images or representations of the objects of external perception. Common sense received directly and unites all the sensations received by all the five external senses, uniting them into one general perception. It perceives each of the sensible particulars, but not intelligible universals. It is able to sense pleasure and pain, both having been perceived in the imagination as well as in the external sensible objects. Common sense gathers together the images or representations that have been sensed, combining them and separating those that are similar from those that are dissimilar in order to make it possible to perceive them, but it does not retain what it receives.

THE POWER OF RETAINING FORMS

The power of retaining of images of physical shapes preserves the sensations of common sense even after the physical form disappears. Its function is to record and retain images or forms of external things received by common sense and to preserve their images and their individual and collective meanings. He says:

> Next is the ability or power of representation located in the rear part of the front ventricle of the brain, which preserves what common sense has received from the individual five senses even in the absence of the sensed objects. It should be remembered that receptivity and preservation are functions of different ability or powers. For instance, water has the power of receiving an imprint, but lacks that of retaining it.[107]

What common sense receives is retained by the retentive power.

THE POWER OF ESTIMATION

The estimative power perceives meanings that are not perceptible to the external senses even though they are within particular sensible objects. According to Avicenna, this is the animal's highest function. In regard to human beings, it is this power that is used in most of our daily relationships and interactions with the world outside of our "self." It is this power that perceives goodness or harmfulness of an object. It is this power that recognizes, for instance, that a fruit is ripe and should be eaten or that so-and-so would make a good partner. This perception is then given to the concupiscent power that is then motivated to move forward or to the irascible power that is then motivated to avoid the perceived harm or pain of it. This is the most important function for animals.

It is through this power that we understand time and space, helping an animal move towards or away from an image. According to Avicenna, while the animal sees the image through this power, it interprets a two-dimensionality as three-dimensional space which is the real situation for the animal and the space through which it has to move.

In other words, it is the estimative power that perceives the individual, non-sensible meaning of sensible particulars, for example, things like love or hate, lust or anger. It is this power that judges concerning right and wrong or good and bad as if the meaning were a sensible object of the world external to "self".

It is this power that perceives intentions as Avicenna explains:

> There are some powers of internal perception that perceive the shape or form of the sensed things, and others that perceive the intention thereof. Some power, again, can both perceive and act while others only perceive and do not act. Some possess primary perception, others secondary perception. The distinction between the perception of the sensed object and that of the intention is that the sensed form is what is perceived both by the inner soul and the external sense; but the external sense perceives it first and then transmits it to the soul, as, for example, when the sheep perceives the form of the wolf, i.e., its shape, form and color. This form is certainly perceived by the inner soul of the sheep, but it is first perceived by its external sense.
>
> As for the intention, it is a thing that the soul perceives from the sensed object without its previously have been perceived by the external sense, just as the sheep perceives the intention of harm in the wolf, which causes it to fear the wolf and to flee from it, without harm having been perceived at all by the external sense. Now what is first perceived by the sense and then by the internal faculties is the sensed object, while what only the internal powers perceive without the external sense is the intention. . . .This estimative power is that judges that the wolf is to be avoided and the child is to be loved.[108]

Avicenna locates this power at the back of the medial ventricle, the place where judgments and opinions are formed. However, unless these judgments and opinions are governed by the intellect and the powers of imagination, this power becomes the source of error in judgment.

It is through this power that the soul is able to deny intellectual images that are not bounded or located. Through it, the soul affirms the existence of a void that encompasses the universe. It is also through it that the soul is able to accept the validity of invalidity of syllogisms that are based on sophistical premises and to differ in the conclusion at which it arrives.

> The estimative faculty presides over judgments not in the analytical way that characterizes intellectual judgments, but in the imaginative way determined by memory images through a process of association from past experience, or not by memory images, but by an instinctive interpretation of the image perceived by the soul without going through any· process of association from past experience.[109]

THE POWER OF MEMORY

It is memory that retains meanings and saves them for the estimative power through which the meanings had been perceived. While the retentive power attains particular meanings and stores them for the person who perceives them for close inspection and appraisal, this only occurs as long as that representative power retains them. When they are no longer available with the retentive power, then they are found in the power of memory. While the retentive power stores sensible images and representations, memory stores meanings and intelligibles.

Memory is, as it were, a treasury or repository for those supra-sensuous ideas discovered by the instinctive ability or power just as the imagination is the treasury or repository for the sense impressions of forms and sensible images (formed by common sense). The place of this ability or power or drive is in the posterior region of the brain.[110]

THE POWER OF IMAGINATION

A fifth internal sense is that of imagination. Avicenna divides this into two parts: sensitive imagination and rational. In comparing power of sensitive and rational, Avicenna states, sensitive relates to one single act while rational does not make a judgment but opens the way to a series of discursive processes and decisions. The power of the rational is concerned with the synthesis and analysis of sense impressions whereas the sensitive power makes a judgment on the super sensuous ideas in the particular sense percepts. The rational is concerned with forms perceived by the senses; the sensitive deals with derivatives therefore (supra sensuous forms).

Avicenna further clarifies the two aspects of imagination, both of which the human being contains while animals only have that of the sensitive. The power is taken in two senses. It is regarded sometimes as 'sensitive' [shared by all animals including the human animal] and sometimes as 'rational' [humans only]. . . .The power of the sensitive or instinct is different than the power of the rational where the rational controls or decides that a given action is advantageous. There is also the difference that the sensitive imagination deals with the senses as well as percepts whereas rational imagination uses the percepts that have been stored in the sensitive imagination and then proceeds to combine and analyze them and construct quite different images, for example, a flying person or an emerald mountain. The imagination does not present to a person anything but what it has already received through the sense-organs.[111]

THE POWER OF IMAGINATION: SENSITIVE

This power receives sensible forms, then combines and separates them through a system of classification. It adds to them or subtracts from them so that the soul can perceive their meanings. In this way, this power connects them with the images. It is naturally disposed to appraise so that the soul can use it to create any order it pleases. It combines and separates objects, adds or subtracts them either through the practical or theoretical intellects. Its main function is to combine and separate rather than to actually perceive something. It is this power that produces technical and artistic skills.

THE POWER OF IMAGINATION: RATIONAL

Avicenna describes the soul's rational imagination as the rational soul, that which separates human beings from animals. It is the cogitative power that manages the data of its two divisions: theoretical and practical intellects, combining and arranging them as premises from which informing knowledge id deducted. From this knowledge, the rational soul derives conclusions. From one conclusion, it derives and combines conclusions and so on.

SUMMARY

Avicenna's identification of the five internal powers is based on three distinct principles of power differentiation.[112]

Avicenna differentiates the powers of estimation and common sense by stating that common sense perceives sensible forms while the estimative power perceives meanings that cannot be perceived by the external senses, but does so immediately by the internal senses. Examples would be, for instance, a sheep perceiving that a wolf is dangerous or a person perceiving that time has passed or whether or not something is good or not good.

He differentiates between those senses that perceive and those that retain what has been perceived. If the same power were to both receive and retain an object, it would have to be moist and dry at one and the same time. As these qualities are opposite to one another, it is impossibility.

He also distinguishes between passive and active powers. Passive powers perceive things as the things are presented to it. Active power can change what has been presented so that there is a perception of something new, different from what was originally perceived.

To summarize Avicenna's descriptions of the five internal senses, common sense perceives images while the retentive power stores them. The power of estimation perceives meanings while memory stores them. The power of imagination both perceives and acts upon the objects.

These internal powers do not relate to any specific sense organ as intermediaries that perform specific functions such as the eyes, or ears and so forth. Rather, the internal powers are of an imaginal and intellectual nature. They do, however, connect with the brain as a physical intermediary. Their various functions are located in the anterior, posterior and middle regions of the brain.[113]

In regard to the soul's consciousness of self (as we will see in the discussion of the human rational soul), this consciousness is not just something intellectual in nature. It involves the power of cognitive imagination and our human ability to reason, as well.

THE WORLD OF IMAGES

In its rational cognitive power of the soul, not its aspect of instinct or fantasy, but its spiritual, intellectual creative imagination that reflects a real world of images, a world that exists independently between the world of matter and the world of ideas and intelligibles.

> This intermediary world reflects realities in the world of pure intelligibles which are, in turn, projected by it in the form of imperfect reflections in the world of sense and sensible experience.
>
> The things in the world of images, which are reflections of realities in the intelligible world, exist in reality, their nature as images being neither purely intelligible nor grossly material.
>
> Images, like those in the dream state, have form and extension and quantity, and yet they are not material; they partake of both aspects of reality, the material and the intelligible, but are in nature neither the one nor the other. They are thus unlike the Platonic Ideas which are pure abstractions of the intellect, the idea of a real world of images (*alam al-mithal*) and the science of symbolism pertaining to the interpretation of the reflections of that world in our world of sense and sensible experience, have their roots in Avicenna (and his mystical treatises). . . .
>
> The imagination that we mean, which is a rational cognitive power of the soul, like intellect, is immaterial, and therefore does not contain the images. When we speak of intelligible forms being 'in' the mind, or

images being in the cognitive imagination, we do not mean that these forms or images are 'contained' in them; it is rather that they are constructions of the intellect or mind during the course of its intellection of them such that they are present to the intellect, and hence referred to as being 'in' the mind; and productions of the cognitive imagination as it involves itself in projecting the sensible world.

In our present state, the intellect's inability to conceive or perceive abstract entities is not due to its essential nature, nor is it due to the nature of the abstract entities, but rather it is due to its own preoccupation with the body which is needed by it as we have mentioned. This being engrossed with the affairs of the body prevents it from perceiving the abstract realities in their original nature because the body acts as an obstruction. When, however, consciousness of the body and of the subjective self or ego is subdued, the intellect will be able to make contact with the Active Intellect and will then be capable of perceiving the abstract realities as they are.[114]

COGNITION
STAGES OF INTELLECTION

There are three possible ways that powers of the soul perform according to Avicenna as the soul is potentially the intellect actualized as intellect by the Active Intellect: potential, possible and habitual power resulting in perfection depending whether they are before or after an action.

Potential power is just that, potential, but capable of receiving effects. It is pure power before an act as, for example, the power in a child to write. As the child grows, this power that was a potential power, through the instrument of actualization is actualized. It is now **possible** for that child to write without the need of any intermediary of a physical instrument, knowing how to use pen and ink as well as understanding simple letters. He now has the ability to write the letters. When the child grows into an adult, the power is completely **habitual** and actualized by the intellect. It is sufficient for the adult to act whenever he or she so desires. The adult now intends the act and acts. The power in the writer has now reached perfection whether writing or not. It is the intellect that is the agent of the power that had earlier on been only a potential.[115]

THE HUMAN RATIONAL SOUL/INTELLECT

The human rational soul is divided by Avicenna into the theoretical and practical intellects.

THE THEORETICAL INTELLECT

The power of the theoretical intellect works in the following way:

If the universal forms are not completely separated from matter, but are separated only in various degrees of separation which still have material connections, such as concepts of objects of the external world or the primary intelligibles (i.e. like the concept of human being as corresponding to a particular, living human being) then it will effect their absolute separation by means of abstraction. If the universal forms are in themselves abstract, then it takes them as they are.

The process of abstraction of sensibles to intelligibles, which is in reality a process devoted to the scope and nature of knowledge that arrives at meaning, undergoes various grades of completion leading to perfection. It begins already in the initial act of perception by sense; then it attains to a slightly higher degree of completion by means of the imagination, and a more refined one by the estimation even before attaining to complete and perfect abstraction by the intellect.

The sensible, particular forms that have already been imprinted in the estimation, imagination, and sensation before the arrival of intelligible, universal forms in the intellect, reside in physical entities representing perceptive powers whose functions are localized in the body. When these forms are present in these powers and are retained by their conservers, they serve as intellectual forms or forms whose complete abstraction requires the exercise of the intellect.

As to the relation of the theoretical intellect to the rational imagination, the contents of the imagination serve the intellect as potential intelligibles, becoming actual intelligibles when the intellect appraises them; not in the sense of being transformed into another form from their state of potentiality in the imagination, or of being transferred therefrom, for they remain as they are in the imagination and maintain their character as images.

Only that when the intellect appraises the images, they produce an effect like the effect that comes about when light falls upon sensible things enveloped in darkness making them visible. Thus the actual intelligibles are something else other than the forms of the imagination, which only serve to generate other forms in the intellect when the intellect appraises them, that is, considers, compares and analyzes them, and then abstracts them from their material attachments and arrives at their universal meanings.

The theoretical intellect first distinguishes their essential natures from their accidental attachments, their similar and dissimilar characteristics, then from the many meanings in the similars it is able to arrive at their single universal meaning; and from the similar meaning in each of the dissimilars it is able to arrive at their multiple meanings. The intellect, then, has the power of deriving many meanings from the single, and a single meaning from the many.

This intellective activity becomes manifest in our formulation of the logical divisions of genus, species, and differentia; the formulation of our syllogisms that enable us to arrive at conclusions and the formulation of definitions.[116]

The activities and relations of the theoretical intellect of the human/rational/cognitive intellect involves four stages whereby this intellect governs intellectual development from potential to actuality, the material, habitual, actual and acquired intellects.

THE MATERIAL INTELLECT

Avicenna states that the material intellect moves from a state of potentially knowing something to an actual state of knowing that. In order to do this, it requires a separate intellect, one that is always active and never potential. This he calls the Active Intellect.

Avicenna explains that the material intellect is like a blank tablet that contains the potential to grasp universals or intelligibles. It is known as "material" not because it is made of matter, but because it acts similar to matter in that it accepts configurations or visible objects.

> This term may imply absolute potentiality in which nothing has yet become actual nor has the instrument of its actualization even been achieved, for instance the capacity of an infant to write.[117]

This intellect is analogous to the Greek concept of primary matter, that is, pure matter that has not been perfected, but is capable of becoming perfected. The difference with the Greek concept is that according to Avicenna, the material intellect is only able to receive perfection that its potential power is able to receive and its potentiality is not the same for all individuals.

> Although the human soul is common in humanity, it differs in potency (Q2:286; Q7:42; Q23:62) and it differs in individuals due to differences in the accidents that make up every personality; and the potential power in the material intellect is therefore not equal in capacity for everyone. The

potency in the intellect is ordered according to nobility of soul, the highest being that of the Prophet.[118]

The Habitual Intellect

In relation to the material intellect, the habitual intellect is active. The material intellect only has the potential power without the ability to act. The habitual intellect brings forth what is potential in the material intellect and has the power to activate it.

> So in like manner does the habitual intellect become actual intellect, and the potential intelligibles become actual intelligibles by means of the light that is shed by the Active Intellect upon the soul. When the intellective power of the soul—that is, the habitual intellect—appraises the particulars in the imagination, this fact of appraisal puts it in a state of readiness to receive the universal intelligibles from the Active Intellect by way of illumination.[119]

It is the habitual intellect that receives first principles that rest on self-evident truths obtained, not by means of deduction nor by verification, but from understanding the truth in the statement that the whole of something is greater than its parts, or that things equal to one and the same thing are equal to one another. It receives these universals from the primary intelligibles.

> It may imply a relative potentiality when nothing more than the instrument of the acquisition of actuality has been achieved. For example; an older child who has learnt the use of the pen and the inkpot and knows the value or meaning of the letters is said to have the capacity of writing.[120]

The Actual Intellect

It is up to the next stage of the intellect, the actual intellect, to not only grasp universals or intelligibles, but to actually be ready to use them.

> It may imply this capacity when the instrument has been perfected, and when by means of the instrument the capacity has been made complete, so that the agent may exercise it whenever he wishes without having to learn or acquire it. The intention is all that is required as in the case of the capacity said to be possessed by a scribe who has reached perfection in his art, even when he is not actually writing.[121]

THE ACQUIRED INTELLECT

Then, the acquired intellect, the highest form of the human state is where the human intellect grows closest to the divine order and the Active Intellect. It is this intellect that makes it possible for the theoretical intellect to understand and acquire universals in the purest form possible.

> At this stage of its actualization it is called the acquired intellect (*al-aql al-mustafad*). It is called acquired because it perceives clearly that when the potential intellect passes over into absolute actuality, it does so by virtue of an intellect that is always in act, and that when this intellect that is always in act makes a specific contact with the potential intellect, it imprints into the latter a specific form, so that the intellect acquires these forms from outside itself.[122]

THE LEARNING PROCESS

Based on the above discussion, the human intellect moves in its intellectual development from potentiality to actuality through stages as Avicenna explains:

> Thus, the relation of the soul's theoretical power to the abstract immaterial forms which we have mentioned is sometimes of the nature of absolute potentiality; this power belongs to the soul that has not yet realized any portion of the perfection potentially belonging to it. In this stage it is called the **material intellect**, a power that is present in every individual of the human species. It is called material in view of its resemblance to primary matter, which in itself does not possess any of the physical forms but is the basis or foundation of all physical forms. And sometimes its relation of the nature of possible potentiality, i.e. when out of its possible perfections only the primary intelligibles which are the source and the instrument of the secondary intelligibles have been acquired by the material potentiality.
>
> By the primary intelligibles, I mean the basic premises to which assent is given, not through any process of learning, nor even with any consciousness on the part of the subject giving assent that it might be just as possible for him sometimes to abstain from doing so, just as we necessarily believe that the whole is greater than the part; and that things which are equal to the same thing are equal to one another. So long as only this amount of actualization has been achieved, it is called the **habitual intellect**; it may also be called the **actual intellect** in relation to the first potentiality, because the latter cannot actually think at all, whereas this

one does so when it begins to reason.

Sometimes its relation is of the nature of perfected potentiality, when, after the primary intelligible forms, it has also acquired secondary ones except that it does not actually contemplate them or return to them; it has, as it were, conserved them, so that it can actually contemplate those forms when it wills and knows that it can do so. It is called **actual intellect** because it is an intelligence that thinks whenever it wills without needing any further process of acquisitions although it could be called potential intelligence in relation to what comes next.

Lastly, its relation to those forms may be of the nature of absolute actuality, as when they are present to it and it actually contemplates and thinks them and also knows that it does so. At this point it becomes the **acquired intellect**, since we shall soon see that the potential intelligence becomes actual only through an intelligence which is always actual, and that, when the potential intelligence makes some sort of contact with it, certain forms are actually imprinted on the former from the latter. Such forms are therefore acquired from without.[123]

Avicenna concludes that these are the four stages of the theoretical intellect. It is by the attainment of the acquired intellect that the human being has potentially perfected self.

He comments on the famous verse of light in the Quran (24:35) as it relates to the the levels of intellectuation. The Quranic verse says:

> God is the Light of the heavens and the earth. The parable of His Light is as a niche in which there is a lamp. The lamp is in a glass. The glass is as if it had been a glittering star, kindled from the blessed olive tree, neither eastern nor western, whose oil is about to illumnate although no fire touches it. Light on light, God guides to His Light whom He wills! And God propounds parables for humanity and God is Knowing of everything. (24:35)[124]

Avicenna's commentary:

> Among the [powers] of the soul, there are those that the soul possesses inasmuch as it is in need of growth and perfection so that it can reach the state of the [**actual intellect**]. The first power is that which prepares the soul for receiving the intelligibles, some call it the [**material intellect**]. It is the *niche*.
>
> Above this ia another [power] that the soul possesses when it has received the first intelligibles and is prepared to receive the second. The second intelligibles can be acquired either by reflection or the intention (which is stronger). The first is symbolized by the *olive tree*, the second

by the *olive oil* itself. In both instances, the soul at this stage is called the [**habitual intellect**], and is like *the glass*.

As for the noble soul that possesses the [**spiritual intellect**], the phrase whose oil *is about to illumnate* hold true for it. It is after this stage that the soul possesses a power and a perfection; and this perfection is that it 'sees' the intelligibles themselves in act, in an intuition that represents them in the mind so that they are manifested to it. The impinging of the intelligibles upon the mind is like *light upon light*. After this is a power that can bring forth and contemplate intelligibles that had been previously acquired by the soul without its having to acquire them anew. This [**acquired intellect**], which is as though illuminated by itself, is like the *lamp*. The perfection is called [**habital intellect**] and the [power, **acquired intellect**].

And that which cause the soul to pass thorugh these stages from the [**habitual intellect**] to the [**acquired intellect**] and from the [**material intellect**] to the [**habitual intellect**] is the Active Intellect, which is like the *fire*.[125]

THE SPIRITUAL INTELLECT

According to Avicenna, it is God Who chooses the prophets. Acting through the Giver of Forms or Active Intellect, the soul of the prophet is prepared to receive revelation.

Avicenna describes the process in the following way:

> The power of imagination is not equal in human beings and differs according to their degrees of intellectual excellence and nobility of soul. In some it is stronger than in others, so that some may be able to see true visions of that intermediary world and others may not. We who affirm prophecy cannot deny the possibility that the forms of the world of images that are reflected in the cognitive imagination may get imprinted in the sensitive imagination to the extent that the perceiver of these forms may actually see them in their sensible guise. Indeed, in the case of the Prophet, for example, his cognitive imagination was so powerful that he was able to perceive intelligible realities in their sensible forms.[126]

THE PRACTICAL INTELLECT

The practical intellect is the cause of movement of the human body that urges it to individual actions characterized by reasoning and deliberation and in accordance with purposive considerations. This intellect regulates the concupiscent and irascible powers as well as that of reason.

The human soul, though independent of the body, yet requires the body in this physical world in order to acquire principles of ideas and be-liefs. By means of its relationship with the body, the rational soul makes use of the animal powers to gain, among the data supplied to it by the senses, the particulars.[127]

The practical intellect seeks knowledge to be able to act with the good in relation to the individual self (body, soul, spirit), society and the state. It must be trained, therefore, to manage each properly. It is described in the sciences of ethics and is to be discussed in the Final Cause. While the the-oretical intellect is oriented upward, the practical intellect is directed down-wards. It looks up to the theoretical intellect and moves the body accordingly. It is the link between the immaterial and material worlds through the power of imagination.

Chapter 3: The Efficient Cause
Introduction

As the Efficient Cause of the soul, in Avicenna's view those things that make up the Efficient Cause play a role in changing the humours of a substantial form including rest or excitability or peacefulness of the body and soul or its motion.

These things bring change in the elemental qualities of some matter, namely, the hot, cold, moist and dry. When the matter has been prepared by these qualities, the Giver of Forms impresses the prepared matter with accidental properties of the matter. It is not that a new substance is brought into being.

The Efficient Cause refers to things other than the soul that bring change or movement to the soul interacting as an agent of the change or movement.

Muslim practitioners recognized six external factors that when healthy affect the soul's powers in a positive way. Avicenna refers to them as the Six Necessities.

1. Air
2. Dietics, Food and Drink
3. Exercise and Rest
4. Sleep and Wakefulness
5. Psychological Factors
6. Retention and Depletion

The practitioner who usually knew his patient well sought to restore health [to the soul] not only by examining internal problems but by studying all the different external factors listed here so as to discover the one or several causes which had disrupted the harmony of the humours within the body and vis-a-vis the environment, causes that can range from having eaten the wrong food to emotional strain.[128]

The Six Necessities

Air

Fresh air is free from pollution with smoke and vapor and it is available in the open rather than in enclosed or covered places. Open air is the best but when the outside air becomes polluted, the inside air is rather preferable. The best air is that which is pure, clean and free from contamination with vapors from lakes, trenches, bamboo fields, saline affected areas and vegetable fields, specially of cabbages and herb rockets. It should not be polluted with the overgrowth of trees especially walnuts and figs.

Once a putrefactive process has begun in the air, it is more likely to continue if the air is free and exposed than when it is enclosed and concealed. Except for that it is better that air be free and exposed.

It is also essential that the air should be open to the fresh breeze and not enclosed. Fresh air comes from the plains and high mountains. It is not confined in pits and depressions hence it is quickly warmed by the rising sun and cools after the sunset. Air would not be fresh if it is enclosed within recently painted or plastered walls. Fresh air also does not produce any choking or discomfort.

Some changes in the air are normal, some abnormal and harmful, while others are neither normal nor particularly harmful. Abnormal changes in the air, whether harmful or otherwise, may or may not be periodical. It is best that a season remain in its own quality rather than be subject to frequent variations which produce disease.[129]

DIETETICS: FOOD AND DRINK

In seeking to maintain health care must be taken that the essential basis of the meal is not in medicinal nutrients like potherbs, fruits, and such-like. For things which are tenuous in character over-oxidize the blood, while those which are dense render the blood phlegmatic and the body heavy.

MENU

The meal should include: (1) meat especially kid of goats; veal, and year-old lamb; (2) wheat, which is cleaned of extraneous matter and gathered during a healthy harvest without ever having been exposed to injurious influences; (3) sweets of appropriate temperament; (4) fragrant wine of good quality.

Any other kinds of food can only be regarded as a sort of medicament or preservative.

The more nutritious fruits are: figs, grapes (ripe and sweet), dates from countries and regions in which they are indigenous. But if superfluity arises after partaking of these fruits, speedy evacuation should be procured.

THE APPETITE

A person should not eat unless hungry. Nor should he delay his meal until the appetite has passed off. This rule does not apply in the case of the fictitious appetite met with in drunkards or the subjects of nausea. If fasting be continued the stomach will fill up with putrescent humours.

HOT MEALS

In winter the food should be hot; in summer cold or only slightly warm. A food should not be served either hot or cold if it is likely to be spoiled thereby.

THE QUANTITY OF FOOD

Nothing is worse than to eat to repletion during a time of plenty after having been in a state of starvation during a time of famine, and vice versa. But the transition period is the worst. For we often see many people who lack food at a time of famine, and eat to repletion when a fertile year comes with fatal result. Great repletion is very dangerous in any case, whether in regard to food or to drink. For how often do not people over-eat, and perish from the consequent choking of the channels of the body?

THE ORDER OF THE MEALS

An error in eating or drinking any of the medicinal nutrients is to be corrected according to the digestion and maturation thereof. The person must be protected from the intemperament which is likely to arise. To effect this, one takes the contrary substance until the digestion is completed.

Thus, if the aliment was cold (i.e., cucumber, gourd), temper it with its opposite (i.e., onions, leek). If the aliment was hot, temper it with the opposite (i.e., cucumber, purslane). If the aliment is binding, take some food which will open and evacuate, and then fast for a suitable period.

A person in this state—and this is true for all who wish to maintain their health—should not partake of food until there is a definite appetite, and unless the stomach and upper small intestine have emptied themselves of the previous meal, because there is nothing more harmful to the body than to superimpose digestive matter upon incompletely digested food.

There is also nothing worse than nauseating indigestion especially when this is the result of bad foods. If these are gross, the following symptoms and illnesses arise: pains in the joints, in the kidneys; difficult or labored breathing, gout of the foot, especially the big toe, hardening and enlargement of the spleen and liver, illnesses in which the serous or atrabilious humours are concerned. If the foods were unnaturally thin, then acute fevers, malignant fevers, and grave acute inflammatory disturbances would develop.

AIDS TO DIGESTION

However, it is sometimes really necessary to give a food or a substance like food, on the top of another food, by way of medicine. For example, if one has taken sharp and salty nutrients, one may further take humectant aliments which have no flavor, before the former have digested completely The chyme by which the body is nourished is then rectified. This is a suitable measure for cases of this kind, and the use of exercise is not indicated. The contrary holds good in the case of those who partake of gross foodstuffs and afterwards admix with them something which is speedily digested and acrid in taste.

FOOD AND EXERCISE

A small amount of movement or activity after a meal allows the food to descend to the fundus of the stomach, especially if after this there is a desire to sleep. Mental excitement, emotion or vigorous exercise hinder digestion.

SEASONS AND FOOD

In winter, feebly nutrient foods like potherbs are not to be eaten. The aliments should be stronger and more solid in texture such as cereals, legumes, and the like. In summer, the contrary is true.

THE SIZE OF MEALS

In regard to the quantity of food taken at a meal, no meal should be bulky enough to completely satisfy the appetite, One should rise from the table while some appetite or desire for food is still present for such remnants of hunger will disappear in the course of an hour. Custom is to be regarded in this regard, for a meal is injurious when it brings heaviness to the stomach, and wine is injurious when it exceeds moderation, and swims in the stomach.

If one ate to excess one day, one should fast the next, and a longer sleep should be taken in some place which is neither hot nor cold. If sleep refuses to come, one should take gentle walking exercise and allow neither rest nor recumbent position. A little pure wine should be taken. Rufus [of Ephesus, late 1st century CE] says: 'Walking after a meal is gratifying to me, for it gives a good preparation for the evening meal.'

FOOD AND SLEEP

A short sleep after a meal is useful; one should lie first on the right side, then on the left, and finally turn back again to the right side. If the body be covered with a number of wraps and the neck be raised, this will aid digestion. The limbs should slope downward and not upwards.

The standard size of the meal depends on usage and vigor. A normally robust person should take as much as will not produce a sense of heaviness, or a sense of tightness of the abdomen. There should be no subsequent rumbling in the stomach or splashing of the food on bodily movement. Nausea should not be experienced, nor a canine appetite, nor loss of appetite, nor great disinclination for exertion, nor sleeplessness. The taste of the food should not repeat in belching. If the taste of food lingers in the mouth a very long time after the meal it shows that the latter was too heavy.

THE QUANTITY OF FOOD

Indications that the meal was moderate: the pulse does not become full; the breathing does not become shallow. The latter only occurs if the stomach is compressing the diaphragm, thus making breathing shallow and short. The pressure to be met by the heart increases after a large meal, and as the force of the heart does not diminish, the pulse becomes large and full.

FOOD AND TEMPERAMENT

The following should be observed: a person who experiences a sense of heat and flushing after a meal should not take a whole meal at one sitting, but partake of the food in small portions at short intervals to avoid the effects of repletion such as shivering followed by a sense of heat like that in a fever producing a high or excessive level of strength and energy. This is due to the heating effect of the food; a person who cannot digest the amount of food appropriate for him should increase the number of articles of diet, but diminish the quantity; a person of atrabilious constitution needs a diet which is very humectant or moisture preserving, but not very heating; a person of choleric constitution needs a diet which is humectant or moisture preserving and cold in nature; a person who generates hot inflammable blood needs feebly nutritious articles of food, which are cold. One who generates phlegmatic blood needs feebly nutritious articles of diet which are hot and blood thinning.

THE ORDER OF THE DISHES

The order in which the components of a meal are to be taken—a person who is desirous of maintaining his health needs to be watchful of this matter. Thus, one should not take a tenuous food, which is rapidly digested, after taking a very nutritious dish which is slowly digested. An exception to this rule has been named above.

The reason is that the first article of food will be digested first and therefore float over the other, unable to enter the blood. Consequently it ferments and decomposes, and in addition sets up decomposition of the food next taken. The reverse order, therefore, is the one to adopt, so that the easily altered food will pass on with the other into the intestine, and then undergo complete digestion.

Fish and similar articles of food should not be taken after laborious work or exercise, because they undergo decomposition and then decompose the humours.

Some persons may be allowed to eat an article of food in which there is a styptic property as a preparatory to the actual meal.

THE PRESCRIPTION OF THE DIET

Some persons have an idiosyncrasy of the stomach in which the foods leave it very rapidly and do not stay in it long enough to undergo gastric digestion. This explains the necessity for taking the idiosyncrasy of the stomach and its temperament into consideration [along with other factors when drawing up a diet].

There are some persons in whom tenuous food, instead of being digested quickly as it should, undergoes decomposition in the stomach, whereas less rapidly digestible foods are digested more readily. The stomach of such a person is designated igneous. But other persons are exactly the opposite. Therefore the rules to be given must be adapted to the peculiarity of each patient.

The countries in which people live have also their own natural properties, which are distinct from the ordinary rule. This must also be borne in mind, and a test must be made to ascertain what the rule should be. Thus, a food which is often used, though injurious to a certain degree, may be more appropriate for a given individual than a food which he does not often take, though its character is good.

Then again, there is a food which is to be regarded as appropriate to everyone's physique and temperament. To change from such a diet would prove injurious and detrimental to him. Good and laudable foods may be injurious to some. They should therefore avoid them. But persons who are able to digest a bad foods should not be deceived, because (for all they know) they will some day give rise to bad humours and the consequent obstinate ailments.

Good food may often be allowed liberally in the case of persons in whom the humours are unhealthy, so long as diarrhea from intestinal weakness does not supervene in consequence. But if the person be of spare habit, and liable to have the motions loose, the diet should consist of moist aliments, because they are digested quickly, even though it is a fact that such persons can tolerate various heavy foods, and are less liable to be affected adversely by intrinsic harmful effects on the body, and are more susceptible to the antagonistic influence of extraneous harmful effects on the body.

THE EXCESS OF MEAT

An active person accustomed to take much meat needs frequent bleeding. A person inclined to be frigid in temperament should drink substances which cleanse the stomach, intestines and the (mesenteric) veins including confections of spices and myrobalan electuary.

It is a bad practice to combine nutrients of diverse character in one meal and so prolong it. For by the time the last portion has entered the stomach, the first portion is already digested, and therefore the various contents of the stomach are not all at then same stage of digestion.

Palatability—one should remember too that aliment is best which has the most agreeable flavor for the walls of the stomach and the retentive faculty jointly apply themselves better to a food of good substance and the efficiency of the retentive power is assisted when the principal members all mutually concur the temperament of one being not more divergent from that of another than natural. That is the requisite condition. The conditions are not fulfilled, for instance, if the temperaments are not normal, or alike in the respective members. Thus, the temperament of the liver may differ to an unnatural extent from that of the stomach. Among noxious influences arising from the taste of aliments is that if very gross aliments are tasty, a person may be tempted to eat too freely of them.

THE NUMBER OF MEALS

In taking successive satiating meals, it is best for a person to take only one on one day and two on the next (morning and evening). But one must not be too strict in this rule, for if a person is accustomed to have two meals a day, and then takes only one, he will be weakened and his digestive faculty will suffer. A person of weak digestion should take two meals a day lessening the amount partaken. On occasion he may eat once a day. A person who is accustomed to take one good meal a day will, on resuming the habit of two meals a day, suffer from weakness, lack of energy, slackness. If he should take no food at bedtime, he will feel weak; and if he should take a late meal he will not be able to digest it, and will have acid belching, nausea, bitter taste in the mouth, loose bowels and become moody, or irritable. This is because he has put into the stomach something to which it is not accustomed, and so he is liable to show some of the symptoms which befall a person whose aliment is not fully digested and these you are now acquainted with.

Among the symptoms arising when a person does not take a late meal are: subjective sensations at the cardiac orifice of the stomach, gnawing pains, a sensation of a void in the stomach so that all the interior organs and intestines feel as if they were suspended and, therefore, all clumped together. He passes scalding urine, and the feces produce a burning sensation as they are passed. There may be a feeling of cold in the extremities owing to the bilious humour being poured out into the stomach and irritating it and making it congested. This is more likely in persons of bilious temperament, and in those who have bilious humour in the stomach but not to an undue extent in the rest of the body; these suffer from loss of sleep, and keep turning over from one side to the other [in bed].

Persons then in whom the bilious humour is apt to accumulate in the stomach should take their meals divided, thereby taking the food quickly; the meal is taken before bathing. In other persons, exercise should be taken first, then the bath, and then the meal. The meal should not precede the bath in these cases. If circumstances demand that the meal betaken before the exercise, the food should consist of bread only, and to an amount no greater than can be easily digested. As it is necessary that the exercise should not be gentle if taken before food, so it is necessary that the exercise should be mild and gentle if it is taken after the meal.

When the appetite is depraved so that it prefers sharp tasting things to sweet or unctuous things, nothing is better than to procure emesis with such as oxymel with radish after fish.

A person who is stout should not eat at once after a bath, but should wait and take a little nap. He is best advised to take only one meal a day.

THE RULES TO BE OBSERVED AFTER MEALS

One should not go to sleep immediately after a meal with the food still swimming in the stomach, and one should, as much as possible, abstain from much exercise after a meal, lest the food pass into the blood before it is sufficiently digested, or glide out of the stomach without being digested at all, or undergoes decomposition, since the exercise disturbs the gastric temperament.[130]

VARIOUS KINDS OF DRINKING WATER

One should not drink water after a meal, for it causes the food to leave the coats of the stomach and float about. One should wait, and not drink fluids until the food has left the stomach which is evidenced by the sensation of lightness in the upper part of the abdomen. However, if there were urgent thirst one may take a modicum of cold water through a straw, and the colder it is the less one will require. Such an amount would soothe the stomach and keep the food together.

To sum up if a person must drink, it is better only to take so small an amount at the end of the meal (not during the meal), as will spread over and moisten the food, and therefore not be injurious.

Water is the only one of the elements which has the special property of entering into the composition of food and drink—not that it is itself nutriment (although it will by itself prolong life for some time), but rather that it enables the chyme to penetrate into the human body and permeate and purify its substance.

We do not wish to imply that water does not nourish at all, but we mean that it is not, as nutriment is, potential blood, giving rise ultimately to body tissue. As an elementary substance, it is not changed in state in such a way as to become able to receive the form of blood or of tissue. This can only occur with a true compound.

Water is really a substance which helps to make chyme fluid and attenuated so that it can flow easily into the blood-vessels and out of the excretory channels. Nutrition cannot be effective without it. It is the handmaid of nutrition.

The various kinds of water differ (1) not merely in the substance of aquosity, but (2) in admixed matters, and (3) their own individual dominant primary qualities.

The best type of water comes from the springs located on a soil which is pure and free from contamination and not from the springs over rocky ground. Although the rocky soil does not putrefy as easily as the pure earthy soil, its water is not as good as that obtained from a pure soil. The water from the springs of a pure soil is, however, not always the best unless it is running and is exposed both to the sun and the air.[131]

EXERCISE, REST AND MASSAGE

The effect of exercise on the human body varies according to its degree—mild or severe, the amount of rest taken, and the movement of the associated humours.

All forms of exercise, whether moderate or excessive, slow or vigorous, increase the innate heat. It makes little difference whether the exercise is vigorous or weak and associated with much rest or not, because it makes the body very hot; but even if exercise should entail a loss of innate heat, it does so only to a small amount. The dissipation of heat is only gradual, whereas the amount of heat produced is greater than the loss. If there be much of both exercise and repose, the effect is to cool the body because the natural heat is now greatly dispersed and consequently the body becomes dry. If the exercise entail the handling of certain material, that material usually adds to the effect of the exercise, although often there is a lessened effect. As an example, if the exercise were in the course of performing the art of the fuller, an increase in coldness and moisture would result. If the exercise were in the course of the performance of the art of the spelter, there would be more heat and dryness.

Rest always has a cooling effect because the invigorating, life-giving heat passes away and the innate heat is confined. It also has a choking and moistening effect because of the lack of dispersal of waste matters.

Since the regimen for maintaining health consists essentially in the regulation of: (1) exercise; (2) food; and (3) sleep, we may begin our discourse with the subject of exercise. We may define exercise as voluntary movement entailing deep and hurried respiration.

Once we direct the attention towards regulating exercise as to amount and time, we shall find there is no need for such medicines as are ordinarily required for remedying diseases dependent on [abnormal] matters, or diseases of temperament consequent upon such. This is true provided the rest of the regimen is appropriate and proper.

We know that this must be so when we reflect how in regard to nutriment, our health depends on the nutriment being appropriate for us and regulated in quantity and quality. For not one of the aliments which are capable of nourishing the body is converted into actual nutriment in its entirety. In every case digestion leaves something untouched, and nature takes care to have that evacuated. Nevertheless, the evacuation which nature accomplishes is not a complete one. Hence at the end of each digestion there is some superfluity left over. Should this be a frequent occurrence, repetition would lead to further aggregation until something measurable has accumulated. As a result, harmful effete substances would form and injure various parts of the body. When they undergo decomposition, putrefactive diseases arise [bacterial infections, Tr.]. Should they be strong in quality, they will give rise to an intemperament; and if they should increase in quantity, they would set up the symptoms of plethora which have already been described. Flowing to some member, they will result in an inflammatory mass, and their vapors will destroy the temperament of the substantial basis of the vital energy.

That is the reason why we must be careful to evacuate these substances. Their evacuation is usually not completely accomplished without the aid of toxic medicines, for these break up the nature of the effete substances. This can be achieved only by toxic agents, although the drinking of them is to a certain extent deleterious to our nature. As Hippocrates says: 'Medicine purges and ages.' More than this the discharge of superfluous humour entails the loss of a large part of the natural humidities and of the vital energy, which is the substance of life. And all this is at the expense of the strength of the principal and auxiliary members, and therefore they are weakened thereby. These and other things account for the difficulties incident to plethora, whether they remain behind in the body or are evacuated from it.

Now exercise is that agent which most surely prevents the accumulation of these matters, and prevents plethora. The other forms of regimen assist it. It is this exercise which renews and revives the Innate Heat, and imparts the necessary lightness to the body, for it causes the subtle heat to be increased and daily disperses whatever effete substances have accumulated; the movements of the body help to expel them conveying them to those parts of the body whence they can readily leave it. Hence the effete matters are not allowed to collect day after day and besides this, as we have just said, exercise causes the innate heat to flourish and keeps the joints and ligaments firm, so as to be always ready for service, and also free from injury. It renders the members able to receive the nutriment, in being free from accumulated effete matters. Hence it renders the attractive faculty active, resolves fibrosis in the tissues, rendering the members light and the humidities attenuated, and it dilates the pores of the skin.

To forsake exercise would often incur the risk of "hectic," because the instinctive drives of the members are impaired, inasmuch as the deprivation of movement prevents the access to them of the innate vital energy. And this last is the real instrument of life for every one of the members.

The value of exercise includes the following: (1) it hardens the organs and renders them fit for their functions; (2) it results in a better absorption of food, aids assimilation, and, by increasing the innate heat, improves nutrition; (3) it clears the pores of the skin; (4) it removes effete substances through the lungs; (5) it strengthens the physique. Vigorous exercise invigorates the muscular and nervous system.

There are two main forms of exercise: (a) that pertaining to the ordinary human undertakings; and (b) that which is undertaken for its own sake— namely, for the advantage accruing from its pursuit. [i.e., sports, athletics, gymnastics, etc.]

There are differences between the two forms. One is strong and powerful, the other weak and light; one is speedy, the other slow. Athletics implies strenuous exertions combining swiftness with energy. Recreative exercise, undertaken for relaxation, implies leisurely movements. There are all grades between these extremes, and there is a mean between them [called moderate exercise].[132]

In regard to massages, Avicenna lists some types: (1) hard massage: this stretches and contracts, and braces the body; (2) soft massage has a relaxing effect; (3) repeated massage diminishes the fat of the body; (4) moderately hard massage; (5) rough massage: this is done with rough towels. It draws the blood rapidly to the surface; and (6) gentle massage is done with the palm or with soft towels. It draws the blood together and retains it in one member.

The object of friction is to render thin persons heavier, and heavy persons thinner; to brace flabby persons, and to modify those who are not pliable enough (giving tone to the body).[133]

SLEEP AND WAKEFULNESS

Sleep closely resembles rest, while wakefulness is akin to exercise and activity. Since both have their own special characteristics, they need separate consideration.

Sleep strengthens the natural energies [digestion of food and elaboration of the digestive products into good blood], by enclosing the Innate Heat within the body and relaxing the powers of sensation [which are asleep]. It does so because it makes the channels of the vital energy moist and relaxed.

Sleep removes all types of lassitude and it restrains strong evacuations. If then followed by appropriate exercise, the power of running is increased unless effete matters accumulate which only the skin can remove.

Sleep sometimes helps to expel these effete matters in that it imprisons the Innate Heat and procures the dissemination of the nutrients throughout the body and the expulsion of the effete matters which are under the skin as well as of those which are deep in the interior parts of the body. These innermost matters push on those which are in front of them in successive waves until they finally reach the subcutaneous tissues and are thereby discharged from the skin. The same action is achieved by wakefulness to a still greater degree, but in this case the effete matter is removed by dissipation, whereas sleep removes it by inducing sweating.

Sleep induces sweating—it does this by a process of overcoming the effete matter and not by a process of continuous dispersal of attenuated matter. When a person sweats heavily during sleep, without obvious cause, nutrients accumulate in excess of the bodily requirements. When sleep encounters matter adapted for digestion and maturation, it turns it into the nature of blood and warms it and in consequence Innate Heat is engendered and travels through and warms the whole body. If there are hot bilious humours and the period of sleep is prolonged, there is abnormal production of heat. Sleeping on an empty stomach produces more dispersion than coldness in the body. During sleep, the indigestible foods, being partially digested, tend to produce coldness. Wakefulness has quite the opposite effect. When the wakefulness is unduly prolonged, it produces disturbance of the brain such as dryness, weakness and impairment of the intellectual faculties or drives.

Wakefulness is, however, however, the contrary way in all these respects. Excessive wakefulness, by oxidizing the humours, produces hot types of diseases. Excess of sleep, on the other, hand dulls the nervous and mental faculty or drives and makes the head heavy. Due to lack of dispersion, cold type of diseases also follow.

Wakefulness increases the desire for food and stimulates the appetite by dispersing the wastes. It, however, impairs the digestion by dissipating the faculties or drives.

A restless and disturbed sleep (insomnia), being in a state between wakefulness and sleep, is bad for all the bodily states.

Undue somnolence entails an imprisonment of the innate heat and makes the body become cold exteriorly. This is why so many blankets are needed to keep the limbs warm during sleep, which are not required in the waking state. That is why the whole body has to be covered up.[134]

PSYCHOLOGICAL FACTORS
HABITS AND ADDICTIONS

Another of the Efficient Causes that Avicenna considers important are psychological factors, particularly emotions, and their interaction with the power of both the Breath of Life and its vital energy in the heart as well as the soul's powers of sensation/perception.

According to Avicenna, a person who has a hot temperament tends to impart heat rapidly; and similarly in the case of cold, rare and dense bodies. The same holds true in the case of internal potencies. This is how it is that a strong character is formed by repeated practice and repeated experience of emotion. It is in this way that moral character is acquired.

Perhaps the reason underlying this, Avicenna states, is that when an emotion appears, it often makes the substance of the vital energy become conducive; and what is suitable for one thing is unsuitable for its opposite. The more often it is repeated, the less does the tendency to the opposite become, for that which is conducive to the opposite, is expelled little by little. It emerges from the aforesaid that a reiteration of pleasure disposes the vital energy to a pleasing state; a reiteration of being sad disposes it to depression.

Some causative agents of enjoyment are powerful, while others are weak; some are known and obvious, others are less known. Among the less known causes are those that have become habits. Things of habit lose their perception.

EMOTIONS AND THE ENERGIES OF THE SPIRIT
EMOTIONS AND THE VITAL ENERGY

Sages and those physicians who agree with them, are satisfied that joy and grief, fear and anger, are passions peculiarly related to the vital energy in the heart.

There is a certain power accruing from every perfected delight. It is the perfection of the given power that produces joy. Happiness implies attaining a goal and the one who apprehends it can only be aware of the delight because he is aware of the change.

As far as quantity is concerned, the more substantial the Breath of Life receiving the pleasure is, the greater is its power. The substance of the Breath of Life is so great that a large part of it is left in its source while another considerable part flows out during the joy that precedes pleasure. However, in the case of scarcity of substance, the laws of physics reserves it and confines it within its source and does not allow it to spread.

In regard to quality, the Breath of Life should be such that it is consistency is excellent so that the luminosity and radiance innate in it would be abundant to the extent that it might be as that of celestial essence.

Such, then, are the various points about the tendency towards pleasure and a feeling of excitement, happiness or elation. Once the general sources of pleasure and the feeling of excitement, happiness or elation are thoroughly grasped, the sources of joy become intelligible, since joy is a form of pleasure.

Avicenna states that is not to be thought that every agent tending towards enjoyment or depression necessarily depends only on the quantity or quality of the substance of the powers of the Spirit or Breath of Life and its vital energy. Other agencies are concerned that act through the agency of factors internal in the vital energy itself. They do this by modifying the temperamental basis or by rectifying the vital energy or by increasing its quantity Thus, they dispose towards enjoyment. On the other hand, an agent of the opposite sign will tend to induce depression.

For Avicenna, the internal factors are traceable to one single source because every act of contrary type, if it be repeated often enough, comes to be more efficient in imparting an effect. Every increment of power carries with it so much more tendency to the accomplishment of the effect. Avicenna adds that this is sufficiently plain from a purely logical point of view.

It is therefore evident, according to Avicenna, that intense enjoyment disposes the vital energy to happiness, grief to depression; that associated depressants do not make an impression on happiness unless they are vigorous; whereas weak stimulants may and do impress themselves thereon. It is, of course, the other way about in the case of depressants.

Avicenna then shows that the increase of pleasure depends on increasing the natural energy and diminishing the vital energy: (1) a strengthening of the natural energy and (2) a diminution of the density of the vital energy—the latter is due to the expansion following enjoyment.

The strengthening of the natural energy is contributed to by three factors, each of which is itself a source of pleasure; (a) the temperament of the vital energy; (b) overproduction of the vital energy beyond that which is lost by dispersal; (c) prevention of excessive dispersal of vital energy in the heart.

The diminution of the density of the vital energy is followed by two things: (i) a tendency towards movement and expansion—this is related to the fineness of its substance; and (ii) an attraction to itself of its own particular nutriment.

This is due to the movement of expansion towards a place away from the movement of the nutriment. This particular attraction is really the natural corporeal tendency to avoid emptiness. In its essence, it is the same with any movement which in itself brings it to pass that the latter things shall take the place of the former. It is the outcome of this law that very distant waters are drawn towards their primary source, and that winds follow the course they do.

It is now necessary to detail the powerful and obvious sources of pleasure. Pleasing influences are things such as: (3) obtaining that which is wished for; (4) satisfying an intention without meeting opposition; (5) preferring to do something peaceful, (6) confidence; (7) the memory of past and future joys and hopes; (8) thinking about ambitious things; (9) mutual argumentation with kindred minds; (10) relief from pain; (11) contact with curious (interesting, unusual, remarkable, new) things; (12) uplifting of the mind; (13) meeting friends and friendly surroundings; (14) overcoming deception in small matters; and many similar things to be found mentioned in books of rhetoric and morals.

Avicenna makes a distinction between weakness of the heart and depression. Weakness of the heart and anxiety, which some people call contraction of the heart are similar and yet there is a difference. The same thing may be said about their opposites: strength of the heart and expansion of the heart. The difference between them is difficult to identify because so commonly one passes into the other.

But there is an obvious difference between the extremes of each as he points out:

(1) Not every weak heart is associated with depression nor is depression always accompanied by a weak heart. A vigorous heart is not necessarily accompanied by joy; and conversely.

(2) The basis is different in each: Weakness of the heart is a disposition assumed in respect of things evoking dread, because it is incapable of tolerating them. Contraction fo the heart, on the other hand, is a condition corresponding to the object causing anxiety because of its inadequacy to bear it. The fearful object is harmful to the body while the object that is causing anxiety is harmful to the soul.

(3) There is a difference in regard to the mental effects. Weakness of the heart impels to defense and to resistance and dissuades one strongly from feeling to escape while anxiety and contraction of the heart impels one to stand still for the purpose of either resisting or repelling.

Weakness of the heart slackens the motivational power of the soul while contraction of the heart stimulates it. Consequently there are two emotions associated with weakness of the heart: (a) that of suffering an injury; and (b) that of the desire to escape.

In the case of anxiety (contraction of the heart) there is just one: that of suffering an injury. In the event of there being a decision to flee, it is because of some contingent circumstance rather than because of an intention to give ground. It is as likely that attack and struggle will be decided upon in place of flight. This desire to escape is voluntary, not instinctive and is often used for offense and resistance.

(4) They differ as to the physical effects on the body. Weakness of the heart and escape from danger are followed by loss of natural heat replaced by cold. Depression, after the particular cause has passed away, is followed by kindling of the natural heat.

(5) They differ in regard to the predisposing causes. Too fine and too cold temperament of vital energy tends to weakness of the heart; coarseness and hot temperament of the vital energy tend to depression.[135]

EMOTIONS FROM EXTERNAL CAUSES
AND THE VITAL ENERGY

When all the conditions required for a given act are present, the slightest agent will now suffice to affect the act. It is because of this that one who drinks wine has a feeling of excitement, happiness and elation to such a point that others think the person is happy without any reason. Such a thing, of course, cannot be. No impression is possible without an impresser.

The fact is that when wine is taken in moderation, it gives rise to a large amount of vital energy in the heart which is of moderate temperament and consistency and whose luminosity is strong and brilliant. Hence wine disposes greatly to happiness and the person is subject to quite trivial exciting agents.

The vital energy now takes up the impression of agents belonging to the present time more easily than it does those which relate to the future; it responds to agents conducive to pleasure rather than those conducive to a sense of beauty. In the same way, its receptivity to the soul's power of imagination is greater than the practical intellect's power of reason.

The reason for this is that the soul requires nervous energy that has a moderate amount of moisture so that it be subordinated to intellectual impetus and the use of reason whereas because of the distraction that wine creates, the nervous energy becomes intensely moist and, as a result, does not submit to reason.

The nervous energy is now impelled by a physical rather than an intellectual or spiritual force. As a result it becomes diffused. At the same time, the vital energy in the heart becomes energized by joy so that intellectual exhilarants do not reach it. Only those energies reach it that lie between sensation and imagination or between sensation and intellect.

In the first case, he says, the vital energy becomes subservient to sensation and is sustained by it. In the second, the power of sensation employs the nervous energy the vital energy is sustained by sensation. Now sensation has a greater control over the energy than the intellect does so that sensation predominates over the inner spirit and energy and is in greater control of its movement.

When the nervous energy disobeys the intellect it is due to the fact that it has been overpowered by the power of sensation. The reason Avicenna gives for this is because the nervous energy is normally able to expel the vital energy when the brain has only a small degree of moisture. The brain at that time has the power to obey the motions of thought and make use of the faculty of understanding.

However, in the case of the external cause of inebriety, an excess of moisture collects in the brain which then prevents the nervous energy obeying understanding and cognition. There are too many ascending and overflowing vapors rendering it too humid. This excess moisture prevents the nervous energy and the power of the rational soul/intellect from reasoning and thinking except in regard to material and sensible objects. It is now unable to consider spiritual matters. Whether moisture is stable or agitated, it cannot take part in the formation or presentation of spiritual issues. It can only respond to sensible or corporeal ones.

The stages in inebriety: The following are the various steps of degradation of the soul, not arranged chronologically: First, recognition of truth is impaired and the operation of the soul is imperfect. The intellectual power falls in proportion. The basis continues to attract vital energy until the temperament of one has reached up to that of the other after which the flow of vital energy, of course, comes to an end.

The power of the vital energy—which is in the 'heart'— has a greater affinity for joy during the state of drunkenness; the happy things that come to it do not reach it by the usual route between the senses and imagination (or even the cogitative power of thinking and reasoning), because the sensitive power has come into dominance.

The repletion of the Breath of Life with Radical Moisture has altered its vigor. The senses now dominate the inner vital energy, and are more powerful than the power of understanding. The power of understanding (as, for instance, for geometry and other exact sciences), meeting as it does a vital energy that is so wanton towards it, unreadily submits to the senses.

Things being so, no wonder that the conception of future, of beauty, of rational affairs, becomes blurred in the intoxicated person's mind; the sense perception of sweet, happy, and delectable things prevails, and the sense of the present is very strong. It is the very strength of this tendency that accounts for the fact that quite a slight agent will evoke happiness and gaiety.

EMOTIONS AND THE POWERS OF THE SOUL
EMOTIONS AND THE HUMOURS

Pure and plentiful blood that is moderate in consistency is conducive to joy since it produces an abundant quantity of vital energy that is pure, brilliant, moderate in consistency and in temperament.

Pure blood which is excessive in heat is conducive to anger because of its inflammation and rapid motion.

Thin, watery, pure, cold blood tends to produce the weakness of the heart and timidity, because the vital energy which is produced from it becomes sluggish in outward movement and slow to inflame because of its coldness. Thus its capacity for joy and anger is decreased, and it becomes both easily soluble due to its thinness, and difficult to dissolve due to its coldness.

· Thick, turbid blood, excessive in heat, predisposes to sadness and fixed and insoluble anger. As regards sadness, it comes from the turbid vital energy generated by the blood; as to anger, it is because the blood, by its heat, becomes highly in flammable. As to enduring anger, it is because the blood is thick. When the object which is tick is heated, it does not quickly cool.

As to the anger born of bilious blood it is liable to be excited and subsides quickly, since the vital energy produced from such blood is more intense in heat, but at the same time it is not dense. And when it is radiant and clear at the same time, it is exceedingly exhilarant.

One who has thick blood, which is not turbid when it has an abundance of heat—which is rare—is far from being sad, and is brave, strong-hearted and less disposed to anger, since cheerfulness is greater than anger. Sadness predisposes to anger, because anger is an act of rejection, while cheerfulness is in relation to pleasure which is an act of absorption. Anger in such a person becomes intensified in his dealings and his vital energy becomes sufficiently thick. Consequently he has little fear.

One who has thick blood, which is not turbid and is abundantly cold, is neither cheerful nor sad nor is his anger intense. His timidity is limited, and he is dull in everything, because his vital energy resembles his blood.

One who has thick, turbid blood with abundance of coldness, is anxious and sad, calm and quiet in anger except in grave situations. His anger is enduring—but of shorter duration than that of the hot-tempered person who resembles him in all characteristics and exceeds that of the person with tender constitution: He becomes a person who wishes to do evil to others.

EMOTIONS AND SENSATION/PERCEPTION

Every form of pleasure results from the perception of perfection that is specific to the soul's power of perception. For instance, the perception of a sweet or sapid taste to the sense of the soul's power of taste or a pleasant fragrance to the soul's power of smell; the awareness of revenge to the irascible power or the awareness of the anticipated benefit innate in the soul's power of imagination.

EMOTIONS AND IMAGINATION

There are causes beyond numbering that incline a person to grief, depression or melancholia. When this occurs, the imagination of the melancholic person heightens and produces images and incidents that increase the sense of desolation and sorrow. In the melancholic person, imagination becomes stronger producing dryness in the constituent temperament of the Breath of Life, slackening its movement and removing the power of reason so that the powers of sensation and imagination prevail because of the disturbance in the temperament of the Breath of Life and its particular movement.

Melancholy persons with confused vital energy remain sad after agencies producing a sense of desolation and grief—such as the following: (1) reflecting that one's homeland is distant; (2) pondering over many injuries already past and done with; (3) hate and rancor; (4) bad health; (5) difficult circumstances of life; (6) thinking terrible things are going to happen in the future; (7) thinking of the necessity for death, which natural judgment ignores because of the obvious fact that we must die; (8) thinking about something that it is disturbing to meditate upon; (9) being away from an agreeable occupation; (10) having thoughts that distract from one's occupation; (11) distraction from that which is desired for and wished for; (12) many other similar things, and others which are beyond comprehension.

Things of this sort easily sadden a mind which is disposed to become sad. Moreover, in melancholy persons, the vividness of the imagination of depressing things itself causes them to appear, because the thing whose image is represented to the mind is already there in actuality. Hence depression persists.

Two things follow great depression: (1) weakening of natural power; and (2) concentration of the vital energy. The explanation of this is that violent condensation and aggregation of the vital energy obliterates the natural heat and results in coldness. Two opposites follow upon this, as has already been intimated.

In addition to a discussion of melancholy and depression, Avicenna notes the role of the soul's power of imagination in one disposed towards taking revenge for a thing. This is related to persistence of anger although there is not sufficient propulsive power to execute the revenge. The anger is neither marked enough nor mild enough. For it must be understood that when anger ceases quickly, the hurtful image does not persist in the imagination, but is quickly subsides and does not produce rancor.

In like manner, too much tendency to secure revenge is countered by two factors: rancor and hate. The one is due to the soul being wholly impelled to revenge, but prevented from continually reflecting upon the hurtful conditions by remembering the things which follow upon having hate fixed in the memory.

The characteristic of the motive power is to divert the soul from its perceptive power and vice versa. What is outside naturally draws attention away from what is inside and vice versa.

Secondly, it must also be remembered that when there is great a tendency to revenge in a fearless person, the impression results as if the imagination had already become possessed of the thing desired for. In aiming at the realization of a power, and hastening towards it, the imagination of such a person turns it into reality. The image is impressed on the imagination as if actually present; then the image of the thing in which the purposed action will end is added to the imagination, and the desire for it ceases to be maintained; the image is abolished, and therefore does not linger in the memory. That is how rancor fades from memory.

When that which exerts a harmful effect on the body is great, as where a sultan or very high dignitary (usually looked on with fear) is concerned, then the fear and anxiety, coupled with the fear together prevent the image of the desire from staying in the rational soul. The result is that the picture of the desire and of that which exerts a harmful effect on the body are both abolished from the imagination, whereas the image of the fear is so much the more dominant to the rational soul that it evokes a desire to flee and not attack. Here again, the image of rancor cannot persist in the rational soul.

When the easily attainable object appears in the imagination as attained, the revenge against the weak appears as realized. The urge for revenge is cancelled from the beginning with the result that it does not develop and ceases to exist.

So, when ease of fulfillment arouses the thought that revenge is attained, the weak-minded person takes it as actually attained. So the love for it vanishes and is entirely obliterated from the rational soul.

Moreover, that the imagination moves according to that which is represented to it and not according to the outcome of things, is shown by the fact that some people dislike honey when it is served up like bilious matter; and they dislike agreeably flavored food should their color be made like repugnant substances: or even when they are served in the appearance of repugnant objects even though such things are not believed to exist at all.

Similarly with this: when a given likeness to the above named thing is portrayed (either because of the intensity of the impulse of the desire, or because of the worthlessness of realizing the desire as though it had actually been attained) it has the same effect as if it had been realized; therefore there is no rancor.[136]

SUMMARY

All these sources of pleasure or harm/pain vary in different races according to their affections, habits and ages. None of them is invariably absent. If two agents usually having a pleasing effect occur together, the effect is not so much the greater. All that happens is that the disposition is more drawn to one than the other. The effect of one only overrules that of the other if the agent in question be very powerful, or, if it be weak, only if it be very persistently at work. This accounts for pleasure being able to persist during the state of inebriation.

Vividness of imagination goes with dryness of the Breath of Life, the movement of which the will has power to correct. Avicenna found that understanding is drawn away from rational actions by the senses and by the imaginings whenever the character of the Breath of Life is perverted; for the Breath of Life moves characteristically towards that direction in which a lack of congenial disposition arises, as when the quality of the Breath of Life is very bad, and when it is confused.[137]

RETENTION (REPLETION)/ EVACUATION (DEPLETION)

RETENTION

The following according to Avicenna are the causes of retention of waste matters: (1) weak expulsive drive; and (2) unduly strong retentive drive. The latter occurs in: (a) weakness of the digestive power so that food remains too long in the stomach, the natural retentive drive holding them back until they are sufficiently digested; (b) narrowness of the channels; and (c) their obstruction; (d) coarseness or viscidity of the waste matter. The former holds in the case of (a) a superabundance of waste matter so that the expulsive drive cannot deal with it; and (b) insufficient informing sense for defecation, this act being aided by voluntary effort. The result may be that the effete matter is compensatorily removed to other parts of the body by the action of the vegetative drives. Thus, jaundice follows [gall-stone] colic; the colic depends on the retention, the jaundice is the compensatory evacuation. Again, at the crisis of a fever, there may be retention of urine and feces, and a critical evacuation occurs elsewhere.

Diseases due to the retention of waste matters are: (1) Compositional such as constipation, diarrhea, or laxity of the bowels, *spasmous humidus* and the like; inflammatory process; furuncles; (2) Intemperaments such as septic conditions; imprisonment of the innate heat, or mutation of this into igneity. There may be so marked a coarctation that the innate heat is extinguished altogether, and coldness of the body supervenes with the transference of too much moisture to the surface of the body; and (3) General conditions: tearing or rupture of locular spaces and crypts.

When repletion (as from great plenty during fertile years) develops after a long period of inanition (as from times of great famine in barren years), it is one of the most effective causes of such illnesses.[138]

EVACUATION (DEPLETION)

In discussing evacuation or depletion, Avicenna says that the causes of the evacuation (depletion) of matters which are normally retained include: (1) Vigorous expulsive drive. (2) Defective retentive drive. (3) Unfavorable quality of the matter which is (a) too heavy, because superabundant; (b) too distending owing to flatulent action; (c) corrosive and acrid in quality; and (d) attenuated of texture, making it too mobile and too easily expelled, and: (4) Widening of the excretory channels. This occurs in the case of the seminal flow. It also occurs if they are torn longitudinally or transversely, or because their orifices become too patent (in epistaxis) from either extraneous or interior causes.

The possible effects of evacuation of this type are: (1) The temperament becomes cold because the matter is lost which would otherwise increase that which maintains the Innate Heat. (2) The temperament becomes hot if the evacuated material is cold in temperament like serous humour or mucus. (3) The temperament becomes equable to blood if there is undue accumulation of the heating bilious humour so that the heat becomes superabundant. (4) The temperament becomes dry. This is always intrinsic in origin. (5) The temperament becomes moist in a matter analogous to that mentioned in regard to accidental increase in body heat, namely, either the evacuation of desiccant body fluid has not been too great or the innate heat is too scanty with the result that the aliment is not adequately digested and serous humour becomes relatively increased. But a moist temperament of this kind is unfavorable to the maintenance of the innate heat and foreign heat will not serve as a substitute for innate heat because of the difference of its nature.

The effect of excessive evacuations on the members of the body include: (1) coldness and dryness of their substance and nature ensue, even though they receive extraneous heat and moisture beyond their need; and (2) diseases from obstruction of the vessels due to undue dryness and narrowing of the veins. Convulsions and tetanic spasms may therefore arise.

When retention and evacuation are equally matched, and occur at the proper times, they are beneficial, and maintain health.[139]

PART THREE: THE FINAL CAUSE:
COMPLETING AND PERFECTING THE SOUL
THE GREATER STRUGGLE

The Final Cause is for the human rational soul to be completed and perfected while it is in the body. The rational soul, as we have seen, has two aspects known as the theoretical and the practical intellects. It is with the activation of these that the human being will be assured of a place in eternity. However, determining that 'place' requires habituating the soul's powers, namely, the power of motivation and its divisions into the soul's concupiscent and irascible powers to moral virtues in order to develop good character.

Avicenna claims:

> The formation of one's moral temperament is based upon whether the practical intellect does or does not successfully act in accordance with these moral judgments in a particular case when there are the passions (i.e., lust and anger or attraction to pleasure/avoidance of harm/pain, concupiscible/irascible power) opposing those judgments.[140]

Good character means habituating the three powers of cognition (reason), affect (concupiscent, lust, attraction to pleasure) and behavior (irascible, avoidance of harm/pain, anger) to moderation and balance. In the view of Avicenna, character is not to be identified with action, a power of the soul or even knowledge. It is the very innate disposition of the soul from which actions emerge. It is permanent, not momentary or accidental.

Training the powers of the soul does not entail uprooting or completely suppressing the powers of the animal soul, which can only occur after death. It does, however, imply their subordination to the practical intellect and reason so that the soul is directed towards the right goal, which is happiness. . . . . . [141]

In Avicenna's short treatise "On the Science of Ethics" he refers to the human obligation to work on one's soul. The process is through:

> . . . .acquiring the virtues which lead to cleansing his human rational soul, and the knowledge of the vices, as well as the means of avoiding them, so that he 'may have achieved for his humanity the perfection leading to worldly and otherworldly happiness.'[142]

Avicenna then gives the principal virtues as temperance, courage and wisdom. Each of these virtues correspond to one of the soul's powers. In other words, attaining these three virtues in by habituating them to balance and harmony. The virtue of temperance arises out of one's completing and perfecting the attraction to pleasure (concupiscent, lust) power. This is done by its submitting to reason, and, according to Avicenna, training concupiscence or lust begins by containing the desire for food and sex.[143]

In regard to seeking pleasure, Avicenna states that it is justified in just three cases:

> Pleasure-seeking is justified, according to Avicenna, in three cases only: (a) restoring the body to health, (b) preserving the individual or the species, and (c) managing the affairs of the state. It is essential, however, that the rational power should constantly superintend pleasurable pursuits and the agent be fully conscious of the end in view, otherwise these pursuits ill turn into occasions for self-gratification.
>
> Two instances are given of the right pursuit of pleasure with the right motive: 'wine-drinking, which is justified for medicinal or hygienic purposes, but not for merry-making,' and music or song, which may be enjoyed for the purpose of 'strengthening the essence of the soul' and reinforcing its internal powers only.[144]

The virtue of courage arises out of ones completing and perfecting the avoidance of pain (irascible, anger) power to reason. The virtue of wisdom arises out of one's completing and perfecting one's cognition, keeping it in balance in the practical intellect which, in turn, submits to the rational soul/theoretical intellect. The theoretical intellect, as we have seen is the Active Intellect. However all of this is voluntary. Avicenna then states:

> Once each of these virtues has attained its perfection or excellence, the fourth, justice, arises.[145]

Avicenna says that justice is the perfection of all other virtues because it is only achieved when each of the other faculties realizes its respective virtue.[146]

Avicenna quotes Aristotle: It is plain that just action is intermediate between acting unjustly and being unjustly treated; for the one to have too much and the other to have too little. Justice is a kind of mean, but not in the same way as the other virtues, but because it relates to an intermediate amount while injustice relates to the extremes.[147]

In addition, Avicenna states that the three virtues of temperance, courage and wisdom consist of multiple sub-virtues. The sub-virtues are to the virtues as the compound of the elements (that is fire being hot and dry, etc.) are to the elements.

> The relationship of the self to the concupiscent and irascible powers (lust and anger) is that certain states arise in it peculiar to the human being by which it is attracted to pleasure or avoiding harm/pain.[148]

According to Avicenna, the attraction to pleasure/avoidance of harm/pain are passive. As such, the practical intellect needs to remain the active disposition within the soul so that it can be completed and perfected.

> This practical intellect, a part of the human rational soul, must govern all the other powers of the body in accordance with the laws of the theoretical intellect empowered by the Active Intellect so that the practical intellect should not submit to these powers, but that the concupiscent and irascible powers [lust and anger] should be subordinated to the practical intellect, lest passive dispositions arising from the concupiscent, attraction to pleasure or irascible, avoidance of harm/pain derived from material things should be stronger. These passive dispositions are those that develop bad morals.
>
> If the concupiscible and irascible powers predominate, then, they are in an active state, while the practical intellect is in a passive one. If the practical intellect predominates, it is in an active state while the animal concupiscible and irascible powers are in a passive one, and this is morals in the strict sense.
>
> If we examine them more closely, the reason why morals are attributed to this practical intellect is that the human rational soul is a single substance which is related to two planes—the one higher and the other lower than itself. It has special powers that establish the relationship between itself and each plane: the practical power that the human soul possesses in relation to the lower plane, which is the body, and its control and management; and the theoretical power in relation to the higher plane, from which it passively receives and acquires intelligibles.
>
> It is as if our soul has two faces: one turned towards the body, and it must not be influenced by any requirements of the bodily nature; and the other turned towards the higher principles, and it must always be ready to receive from what is there in the Higher Plane and to be influenced by it. So much for the power of the Practical Intellect.[149]

In the *Kitab al-Shifa* Avicenna states that one should maintain the mean, the balance, moderation, between any two negative traits. That is, the soul should be maintained in balance between too much or too little of a positive trait as too much or too little indicates a negative. This, according to Avicenna, is the way to acquire and maintain balance.

Vices, in his view, result when the passions dominate reason or the practical intellect and reason is ignored.

> For Avicenna, then, vice is a decided deficiency of the proper human perfection, namely, the activity of the intellect, for in acting viciously one rejects the conclusions of the human intellect in prefrerence for irrational bodily desires.[150]

Avicenna clearly states in the *Kitab al-Shifa* that too much or too little of a positive trait are negative traits. They are the necessary consequence of the soul's animal power of attraction to pleasure and avoidance of harm/pain having ensouled our body.

The reason why the soul wants to attain balance is so that it:

> . . . .transcend the conditions that tie us to the body and preserve the proper state of the human rational soul, while so preparing the human rational soul to go beyond and transcend the body.[151]

According to Avicenna, this is the right inclination or impetus of the human soul in order to attain for it to attain its completion and perfection. Attaining this involves a struggle as the power of the rational soul is constantly being overpowered by the motivational powers of the animal soul. As we have seen, when this happens the soul begins taking on negative traits, preventing the rational soul from perfection.

To the extent that the rational soul and its power of reasoning attains balance, the rational soul is being prepared for its separation from the body. Therefore, when the irrational passions dominate the practical intellect and reason is ignored, negative traits develop.

Avicenna then describes the various sub-virtues of the leading ones of temperance, courage and wisdom:

> The subdivisions of temperance, or the virtue of the concupiscent power, are generosity and contentment; those of courage, the virtue of the irascible, are steadfastness, patience, forgiveness, pardon, broadmindedness, moral stamina, and keeping confidences; those of wisdom, the virtue of the rational, are eloquence, keenness, sagacity, firmness,

truthfulness, loyalty, friendliness, mercifulness, modesty, promise-keeping and humility.[152]

[Avicenna] then proceeds to define the main virtues listed above.

Temperance consists in curbing the passions by subordinating the concupiscent power to the rational; contentment in refusing to occupy oneself with the unnecessary or superfluous, in matters of provision, or to take any notice of the possessions of others.
Courage consists in training the irascible power to put up with pain or hardship.[153]

A key virtue is that of moral stamina, which, although somewhat elusive, is affiliated to the virtue of courage. [Avicenna] defines it:

. . . .as imperturbability in face of passion or anger, whereby the human being's 'pure essence' is not allowed to be swayed or his mind diverted from the thought of the intelligible and divine worlds.[154]

The human rational soul then dwells on the thought of the Spirit and puts aside vain pursuits in both word and deed. The soul then concentrates and focuses on fairness and justice to the extent that it becomes an ingrained habit in the soul.

A logical consequence of this virtue is wisdom, manifested in concern for the welfare of others, affection for those who are virtuous, and a sincere desire to deter and reform the wicked. It is moreover attended by the constant thought of immortality and an unruffled attitude towards death.
Finally, the virtuous human being will not be delinquent in performing his religious duties, or honoring the divine laws or observances. When he turns inwards, his mind will be occupied exclusively with the thought of the First King and His Kingdom, and his soul will be swept of the 'dust of [humanity],' without his fellowmen's knowledge. Whoever has pledged himself to lead this mode of life and to adopt this religious code, will be assisted by God to achieve success in whatever he undertakes.[155]

The concept of equilibrium or justice as the necessary condition for the wedding of the soul and the mixture of the elements is widespread in Islam and is far from being confined to [Avicenna].
According to this view, once the harmony and correct proportion of

the elements has been reached, the soul cannot but be attracted toward it because of the inner sympathy which exists between the invisible and the visible.

Justice, the mean, equilibrium, harmony, are so many expressions of the same basic idea that dominates the universe and preserves the wedding of 'heaven' and the 'earth'. It is the mingling of substances in the compound bodies that accounts for their ability to receive life. The commingling of the components so modifies their contraries as to produce an ensemble in which all the various contraries are blended harmoniously.

The more harmonious the blending, the more suitable is the resultant compound to be the vehicle, not merely of life in general, but of a very particular kind of life. Perfect equilibrium and perfect balance render possible the manifestation of the perfect intellectual life that celestial beings possess but which may be also enjoyed by the human being.[156]

SOCIAL PSYCHOLOGY

Avicenna also wrote on the importance of social psychology. In the *Kitab al-Shifa*, he states that in order for a society to achieve a state of justice, there needs to be a ruler or leader who enforces moral discipline through promoting the virtues of temperance, courage and wisdom, the balance of which results in justice. In dealings with each other, the virtuous member of such a society will then:

> . . . .approach another according to the latter's personal mood, i.e. the serious in a spirit of serious-mindedness, the frivolous in a spirit of frivolity, while guarding his own inner state concealed from his fellows. He will assist the needy with discretion, honor his pledges and refuse to resort to oathmaking.
>
> Thus, the moral judgments can and do function like general rules by which one might flourish in a society. The practical intellect in turn takes these general moral claims and applies them to the particular day-to-day cases with which we find ourselves confronted in order to determine whether to proceed or to avoid some particular line of action, whether the action is beneficial or harmful, as well as whether the particular action is morally good or bad.[157]

Avicenna points to the importance and usefulness of the acts of worship in sustaining society's remembrance of God and the resurrection in the hereafter which are essential for the continuance of political life.[158]

To this Avicenna adds the importance of one following the Prophet's characteristics:

> . . . .the human being in whom it [the prophet's characteristics] is embodied will almost be a human lord and his worship next to God Almighty will be almost lawful. Such a person is the sovereign of the world and God's vicegerent thereon.[159]

PART FOUR: CONCLUSION
CRITICAL THINKING
INTRODUCTION

There are two basic ways of acquiring knowledge according to Islamic teachings. One is through knowledge that is transmitted where one imitates or follows an authority (*taqlid*) and the other is thought-based knowledge, knowledge that one verifies and realizes for oneself (*tahqiq*) whereby one becomes a *muhaqqiq*. It is this latter type of acquiring knowledge that is central to a living intellectual tradition. It has been shown that no religion throughout history can flourish or even survive without this.

> The correct exercise of reason in Islam is tied to personal conviction as opposed to indiscriminate following of others, hallowed custom, and precedent. These must be judged in the light of reason and abandoned if found deviant and misleading. Indiscriminate imitation of others is widely held to be the single most damaging cause of the decline of creative thinking among Muslims.[160]

We naturally learn language, culture, revealed texts, ritual and the Divine Law through imitation. In the case of intellectual or thought-based knowledge, however, one cannot, for instance, learn mathematics because someone said that two plus two equals four. We have to understand it for ourselves, be awakened to it.

> This becomes clear as soon as we ask ourselves the questions: What was the intellectual tradition for? What function did it play in society? What was its goal? In other words: Why should people think? Why shouldn't they just blindly accept whatever they're told? The basis Muslim answer is that people should think because they must think, because they are thinking beings. They have no choice but to think, because God has given them minds and intelligence. Not only that, but in numerous Quranic verses God has commanded them to think and to employ their intelligence. To think properly a person must actually think, which is to say that conclusions must be reached by one's own intellectual struggle, not by someone else's.[161]

Avicenna showed himself to be a critical thinker, known as a *muhaqqiq* in the Islamic world, that is, one who realizes and verifies intellectual knowledge. Based on his ability to think independently, he has many firsts including the fact that he is the central figure in history to develop the Radical Moisture concept and the role it plays in living a healthy life. In *The Canon of Medicine,* he is the first to describe the methods of agreement, difference and concomitant variation that are critical to the scientific method and inductive logic. In the same work, he recognizes and provides treatment for insomnia, mania, vertigo, paralysis, stroke, epilepsy, depresson and male sexual dysfunction, being as he was "a pioneer in the field of psychosomatic medicine, linking changes in mental state to changes in the body.[162]

In addition, examples of his critical thinking are his ability to analyze and evaluate arguments; to make interdisciplinary connections; to make plausible inferences; to think precisely about thinking and to think independently. His focus in doing this was not on the practical affairs of the world, but rather on the complete realization of human intelligence. This demanded that he discover the reality of things, their truth, as well as to act in accord with that.

ANALYZING OR EVALUATING ARGUMENTS, INTERPRETATIONS

Avicenna applied a principle that was unique to him in analyzing the difference between how the external and internal senses receive cognitive objects using tools to understand the reasoning behind something. Independent thinkers like Avicenna develop their own theories, having first verified them.

He recognized that sensible forms are those objects of perception that the external senses grasp immediately. Then, through them, the sensible forms are perceived by the internal senses. Judgment, meaning and intention, however, are not at all perceived by the external senses, but immediately by the internal senses. Examples would be a sheep perceiving that a wolf was a danger or someone sensing that time has passed or whether or not something is good or bad. The ability to judge something is a non-sensible quality that is inherent in material things. Avicenna was in this way to differentiate between powers of the soul, namely, between the power of common sense that perceives sensible forms and the power of estimation that perceives meaning, purpose and intention and is able to make a judgment.

MAKING INTERDISCIPLINARY CONNECTIONS

For Avicenna and other medieval philosophers, psychology is placed under the science of natural science and the study of physics. When considering topics that transcend a particular subject, he brings relevant concepts—i.e., motion—as well as knowledge and insight from many different sciences. Natural science for Avicenna is the study of bodies and how they undergo motion or change. He identifies psychology and the study of the soul with other sciences that study living bodies, their distinction from non-living bodies is that they move and change.

MAKING PLAUSIBLE INFERENCES

It was clear to Avicenna that the soul completes and perfects the body with regard to its species. Since a particular soul belongs to a particular body and it perfects the existence of that body, whether it is a specific plant or animal, its soul belongs to it. Avicenna argues that the soul is either the material cause of the body, that cause by which it is in potency, or the formal cause of the body, that cause by which the potency is made actual.

> There can be no doubt that the body is that through which the living thing is what it is potentially. Now, if the soul likewise were merely something by which a living body is what it is potentially, then the soul would not in fact complete and perfect the living thing insofar as it is plant or animal. That is because it is not merely potentially being able to perform the various activities that completes and perfects the plant or animal but actually being able to perform those activities. Hence, if the soul only explained the living body's potential capacity to perform the activities associated with life—in other words, if the soul were simply the material principle of the body—there would need to be yet another principle that explains the actual capacity to perform those activities. Yet, as has been seen, the soul is the very principle that explains the actual performance of those activities. Thus, the soul cannot be the material principle of a living body. Therefore the soul is a perfection.[163]

THINKING PRECISELY ABOUT THINKING

The highest perfection of the soul for Avicenna is to transform it into the intellect—the rational intellect in both its theoretical and practical aspects, the theoretical being actualized by the Active Intellect. It is through this that one is able to engage in metacogniton, that is, to think about thinking, to know things that are immaterial that do not require matter for their being. According to Avicenna, the reason many human beings do not reach this level of perfection is due to their attachment to matter and the material world.

He says: "In self-awareness, the soul conceptualizes itself, and in so doing makes itself the act of the intellect, an intellect, and an object of the intellect." (Avicenna, *Kitab al-Shifa,* Psychology, V.6, 239.7-8) Since the object of thinking is the intellect thinking about itself thinking, this is perceiving oneself as an immaterial substance. According to Avicenna, this is the complete identification of knower, object known and the act of knowing.

This introspection is the essence of Avicenna's famous argument about "the Flying Person."

> One of us must suppose that he was just created in an instant, fully developed and perfectly formed but with his vision shrouded from perceiving all external objects—created floating in the air or in space, not buffeted by any perceptible current of the air that supports him, his limbs separated and kept out of contact with one another, so that they do not feel each other. Then let the subject consider whether he wo
> uld affirm the existence of his [rational soul].
>
> There is no doubt that he would affirm his own existence, although not affirming the reality of any of his limbs or inner organs, his bowels, or heart or brain, or any external thing. Indeed he would affirm the existence of this [rational soul] of his while not affirming that it had any length, breadth or depth. And if it were possible for him in such a state to imagine a hand or any other organ, he would not imagine it to be a part of himself or a conditions of his existence.
>
> But you know that what is affirmed is distinct from what is not affirmed, and what is implied is distinct from what is not implied. Thus the self, whose existence he affirmed, is his distinctive identity, although not identical with his body and his organs, whose existence he did not affirm.
>
> Accordingly, one who directs his thoughts to this consideration has a means of affirming the existence of the [rational] soul as something distinct from the body, indeed, as something quite other than the body, something which he knows through his own self-consciousness, even if he had overlooked it and needs to be alerted to it.[164]

Based on this experiment, Avicenna could say: Inasmuch as I am aware of having any experience, I am aware that I am the one having it. Thinking about thinking, one becomes indistinguishable from intelligence.

The self knows that it is not limited by the objects of its knowledge or by the finiteness of things, nor by the limitations of this standpoint or that science; it also knows that it has the potential to perceive and comprehend all definitions and all limitations. Hence it knows—if it is self-aware—that it has no inherent limitations. It knows that it is free, not of this or that, but of all things, of everything other than the Real.[165]

THINKING INDEPENDENTLY

As an independent thinker, Avicenna incorporates all known relevant knowledge and insight into his arguments that are in accord with his belief system. Avicenna speaks to how our material intellect moves from potentially knowing something to actually knowing it. He argues that such a movement requires a separate intellect that is always in a state of actuality and never potential. This cause he calls the Active Intellect. As in many other areas of his psychology, once again Avicenna shows his independent thinking and unique understanding of the key points that explain the Active Intellect. In this case it is through his concept of light and vision.

> The eternal light of God is a permanent presence in the created order. The reverberation of this light in human experience is called intellect or spirit or heart. All things are known to this light because it is the conscious and aware pattern in terms of which both the universe and human beings came into existence.[166]

Avicenna's understanding of the role that light plays in the Active Intellect is solely that of his own. He writes:

> The human soul is at one time potentially intellecting and thereafter comes to be intellecting actually. Now, whatever emerges from potency to act does so only by means of a cause in act that brings about its emergence. So, in the present case there is a cause that brings about our souls' emergence from potency to act with respect to the objects of intellection. Since it is the cause providing the intellectualizing forms, it is nothing but an Active Intellect in whom the principles of the intellectualizing forms are separate.[167]

Avicenna then describes how the Active Intellect functions to bring about intellectual perception.

> [The Active Intellect's] relation to our souls is that of the Sun to our vision. Now, just as the Sun is actually visible in itself and through its radiant light (*nur*) it makes actually visible what is not actually visible, so

likewise is the state of this intellect vis-a-vis our souls.

[That] is because when the intellectual faculty reviews the particulars that are in the retentive imagination, and the Active Intellect radiates its light into us [and] upon them, the things separated from matter and its (phenomena that naturally accompanies or follows something) are altered and impressed upon the rational soul. [Being altered is here] not in the sense that [the particulars] themselves are transferred from the (synthetic) imagination to our intellect, nor [is being impressed] in the sense that the meaning immersed in the [material] (phenomenon that naturally accompanies or follows something) which in itself and with regard to its very being is separate [from matter]—makes something like itself.

Quite the contrary, [being altered] and [being impressed] are in the sense that reviewing [the particulars] prepares the soul in order that the thing separate from matter [coming] from the Active Intellect [that is, again, the intellectualizing forms] emanates upon them.

Discursive thought and selective attention are then certain motions that prepare the soul to receive the emanation. This is like [how] middle terms prepare [the soul] to receive the conclusion in the most convincing way, although the first is according to one way and the second according to another, as you will come to know.

So when a certain relation to this form falls to the rational soul by means of the Active Intellect's radiant activity, then from [the relation] there comes to be in [the human soul] something that in one way is of the genus of [the form] and in another way is not. Just like when luminous light falls on colored objects, it produces from them an impression on the visual system that is not in every way reduced [to their sum], so likewise the images that are potentially intelligible become actually intelligible— not themselves but what is acquired from them.

In fact, just as the impression of the sensible forms conveyed by means of luminous light is not itself those forms, but rather something related to them that is engendered by means of the luminous light in the recipient facing [the light], so likewise when the rational soul reviews those forms in the retentive imagination and the radiant light of the Active Intellect comes into a type of contact with them, then they are prepared so that from the luminous light of the Active Intellect they come to be the abstract version of those forms free from material taints within the rational soul.[168]

For Avicenna it was clear that to Avicenna God is One and He is the source of reality and truth, the Origin and Return of all things as he clearly states:

Knowers desire the Real, the First, only for His sake, not for the sake of something else. They prefer nothing to true knowledge of Him. Their service is directed only to Him, because He is worthy of service, and service is a noble relationship with Him. At the same time, knowers have neither desire nor fear. Were they to have it, the object of desire or fear would be their motive, and it would be their goal. Then the Real would not be their goal but rather the means to something less than the Real, which would be their goal and object.[169]

Thinkers like Avicenna analyzed the souls of plants, animals and human beings inorder to integrate everything of the creation into the vision of *tawhid*, asserting the unity of God.

ENDNOTES

Avicenna. (1906). *Qasida al-Ainiyya (Ode to the Soul)*, pp. 110-111. Translated by E. G. Browne, *A Literary History of Persia*.

2 Seyyed Hossein Nasr. (1976). *Three Muslim Sages*, pp. 20-22.

3 Jon McGinnis. (2010). *Avicenna*, p. 228.

4 Seyyed Hossein Nasr. (1976). *Islamic Science: An Illustrated Study (ISIS)*, p. 159.

5 Jon McGinnis. (2010). *Avicenna*, p. 227.

6 Avicenna. (1997). *Qanun fil Tibb (The Canon of Medicine) (TCM)*. Adapted by Laleh Bakhtiar, vol. 1, p. cxvi.

7 Jon McGinnis. (2010). *Avicenna*, p. 228.

8 Jon McGinnis. (2010). *Avicenna*, pp. 228-229.

9 Ehsan Yarsharter, ed. (1996-) *Encyclopedia Iranica*. Online Version.

10 Peter L. Lutz. (2002). *The Rise of Experimental Biology: An Illustrated History*, p. 60.

11 Amber Haque. (2004). "Psychology from an Islamic Perspective: Contributions of Early Muslim Scholars and Challenges to Contemporary Muslim Psychologists". *Journal of Religion and Health* 43 (4): 357-377 [376] (AH).

12 Amber Haque. (2004). (AH), 43 (4): 357-377 [376].

13 Amber Haque. (2004). (AH), 43 (4): 357-377 [376].

14 Jon McGinnis. (2010). *Avicenna*, p. 90.

15 Avicenna. (2010). *Kitab al-Najat*, "Psychology", 1, 318.2-4. Jon McGinnis, (JM), p. 92.

16 R.J. Hankinson. (2009). "Medicine and the Science of the Soul," *Can Bull Med Hist*. 26(1):129-154.

17 Seyyed Hossein Nasr. (1993). *Introduction to Islamic Cosmological Doctrines (ICD)*, p 215.

18 Seyyed Hossein Nasr. (1976). *(ISIS)*, p. 160.

19 Seyyed Hossein Nasr. (1976). *(ISIS)*, p. 159.

20 Avicenna. (1331/1952). *Danishnamah-yi Ala al-Dawlah* (Book of Science Dedicated to Ala al-Dawlah), *Ilahiyat*, pp. 134-135. Seyyed Hossein Nasr, *(ICD)*, p. 240.

21 Avicenna. (1331/1952). *Risalah Dar Haqiqat wa Kaifiyat-i Silsila-yi Mawjudat wa Tasalsul-i Asbab wa Musabbabat*, pp. 24-25. Seyyed Hossein Nasr, *(ICD)*, pp. 206-207.

22 See Avicenna. (1997). *Qanun fil Tibb (The Canon of Medicine) (TCM)*. Adapted by Laleh Bakhtiar, vol. 1, §21-§24.

23 See Avicenna. (1997). *Qanun fil Tibb (The Canon of Medicine) (TCM)*. Adapted by Laleh Bakhtiar, vol. 1, §486-§488.

24 Jalal al-Din Rumi. (1906). *Masnavi*, 3:218. Translated by E. G. Browne, *A Literary History of Persia*.

25 Avicenna. (1952). *Kitab al-Najat: Avicenna's Psychology: An English Translation of Kitab al-Najat, Book, II, Chapter VI with Historico-Philosophical Notes and Textual Improvements on the Cairo Edition*, pp. 56-58. Translated by

Fazlur Rahman (FR).

26 Avicenna. (1952). *Kitab al-Najat*, p. 109. Fazlur Rahman, (FR).

27 Avicenna. (1952). *Kitab al-Najat*, p. 56. Fazlur Rahman, (FR).

28 Jalal al-Din Rumi. (1898). *Divan-e Shams-e Tabrizi*, p. 338. Translated by R. A. Nicholson.

29 Avicenna. (1952). *Kitab al-Najat*, pp. 54-55. Fazlur Rahman, (FR).

30 Avicenna. (1952). *Kitab al-Najat*, p. 57. Fazlur Rahman, (FR).

31 Avicenna. (2010). *Kitab al-Shifa*, "Psychology", I.16.13-17. Jon McGinnis, (JM), p. 94.

32 Avicenna. (2010). *Kitab al-Shifa*, "Psychology", I.1, 12:6-8. Jon McGinnis, (JM), p. 93.

33 Avicenna. (2010). *Kitab al-Shifa*, "Psychology", I.1, 11.7-10. Jon McGinnis, (JM), p. 93.

34 Seyyed Hossein Nasr. (1993). (*ICD*), pp. 245-246.

35 Avicenna. (1952). *Kitab al-Najat*, pp. 24-25. Fazlur Rahman, (FR).

36 Seyyed Hossein Nasr. (1993). (*ICD*), p. 249.

37 Seyyed Hossein Nasr. (1993). (*ICD*), p. 249.

38 Avicenna. (1952). *Kitab al-Najat*, p. 25. Fazlur Rahman, (FR).

39 Avicenna. (2010). *Kitab al-Shifa*, "Psychology", 231.3-233.5. Jon McGinnis, (JM), p. 129.

40 Avicenna. (2006). *Kitab al-Shifa*, "Psychology", Ii. Lenn E. Goodman, *Avicenna*, (LG) p. 155. Dr. Goodman uses "self" in this quote, referring to the rational soul.

41 Avicenna. (2006). *Kitab al-Isharat wal Tanbihat* III 1, 2:319-24. Lenn E. Goodman, (LG), pp. 157-158.

42 Jon McGinnis. (2010). *Avicenna* (JM), p. 143.

43 Avicenna. (1952). *Kitab al-Najat*, pp. 55-56. Fazlur Rahman, (FR).

44 Avicenna. (1952). *Kitab al-Najat*, p. 38. Fazlur Rahman, (FR).

45. Avicenna. (1990). *Kitab al-Shifa*, pp. 212-220. Translated by Syed Naquib al-Attas. *The Nature of Man and the Psychology of the Human Soul* (*NHS*), p. 25.

46 Avicenna. (1952). *Kitab al-Najat*, pp. 35-36. Fazlur Rahman, (FR).

47 Avicenna. (1952). *Kitab al-Najat*, p. 36. Fazlur Rahman, (FR).

48 Avicenna. (1952). *Kitab al-Najat*, p. 37. Fazlur Rahman, (FR).

49 Avicenna. (2010). *Kitab al-Shifa*, "Psychology", V.6, 248.9-250.4. Jon McGinnis, (JM), pp. 147-148.

50 Avicenna. (1990). *Kitab al-Shifa*, p. 185; *Kitab al-Najat*, pp. 202-203. Syed Muhammad Naquib al-Attas, (*NHS*), p. 16.

51 Avicenna. (1997). *Qanun fil Tibb* (*The Canon of Medicine*). (*TCM*). Adapted by Laleh Bakhtiar, §15.

52 Mahmud Shabistari. (1923). *Gulshan-i Raz*, lines 250-255. Translated by E. H. Whinfield.

53 Seyyed Hossein Nasr. (1993). (*ICD*), p. 241.

54 Avicenna. (1993). *Kitab al-Shifa, Tabiiyat*, p. 145. Seyyed Hossein Nasr (*ICD*), p. 241.

55 Avicenna. (1993). *Danishnama-yi alai, Tabiiyat*, p. 53. Seyyed Hossein

Nasr, (*ICD*), p. 216.

56 Seyyed Hossein Nasr. (2001). *Science and Civilization in Islam* (*SCI*), pp. 219-220.

57 Seyyed Hossein Nasr. (1976). (*ISIS*), p. 161.

58 Avicenna. (1997). See *Qanun fil Tibb* (*The Canon of Medicine*) (*TCM*). Adapted by Laleh Bakhtiar, §91-§95.

59 Avicenna. (1997). See *Qanun fil Tibb* (*The Canon of Medicine*) (*TCM*). Adapted by Laleh Bakhtiar, §78.

60 Avicenna. (1997). See *Qanun fil Tibb* (*The Canon of Medicine*) (*TCM*). Adapted by Laleh Bakhtiar, §79-§90.

61 Avicenna. (1997). See *Qanun fil Tibb* (*The Canon of Medicine*) (*TCM*). Adapted by Laleh Bakhtiar, §96-§107.

62 Avicenna. (1997). See *Qanun fil Tibb* (*The Canon of Medicine*) (*TCM*). Adapted by Laleh Bakhtiar, §53.

63 Avicenna. (1997). See *Qanun fil Tibb* (*The Canon of Medicine*) (*TCM*). Adapted by Laleh Bakhtiar, §54.

64 Avicenna. (1997). See *Qanun fil Tibb* (*The Canon of Medicine*) (*TCM*). Adapted by Laleh Bakhtiar, §55.

65 Avicenna. (1997). See *Qanun fil Tibb* (*The Canon of Medicine*) (*TCM*). Adapted by Laleh Bakhtiar, §56.

66 Avicenna. (1997). See *Qanun fil Tibb* (*The Canon of Medicine*) (*TCM*). Adapted by Laleh Bakhtiar, §33-§37.

67 Avicenna. (1997). See *Qanun fil Tibb* (*The Canon of Medicine*) (*TCM*). Adapted by Laleh Bakhtiar, §39-§43.

68 Avicenna. (1997). See *Qanun fil Tibb* (*The Canon of Medicine*) (*TCM*). Adapted by Laleh Bakhtiar, §44.

69 Avicenna. (1997). See *Qanun fil Tibb* (*The Canon of Medicine*) (*TCM*). Adapted by Laleh Bakhtiar, §45.

70 Avicenna. (1997). See *Qanun fil Tibb* (*The Canon of Medicine*) (*TCM*). Adapted by Laleh Bakhtiar, §46-§50.

71 Robert Hall. (2004). "Intellect, Soul and Body in Ibn Sina," Jon McGinnis, ed. *Interpreting Avicenna: Science and Philosophy in Medieval Islam,* (RH) p. 66.

72 Robert Hall. (2004). (RH), p. 66.

73 Jon McGinnis. (2010). (JM), p. 88.

74 Jon MCGinnis. (2010). (JM), p. 135-136.

75 Avicenna. (1990). *Kitab al-Shifa*, p. 208; *Kitab al-Najat*, p. 231. Syed Muhammad Naquib al-Attas, (*NHS*), p. 27.

76 Avicenna. (1952). *Kitab al-Najat*, p. 31. Fazlur Rahman, (FR).

77 Avicenna. (1990). *Kitab al-Najat*, p. 68. Syed Muhammad Naquib al-Attas, (*NHS*), p. 24.

78 Jon McGinnis. (2010). (JM), p. 132.

79 The Breath of Life, manifesting itself through the vital energy, is a kind of subtle body that penetrates all parts of the material body and infuses it like the perfume of a rose, oil in sesame, butter in milk.

80 Avicenna. (1997). See *Qanun fil Tibb* (*The Canon of Medicine*). (*TCM*).

Adapted by Laleh Bakhtiar, §485-§486.

81 Avicenna. (1997). See *Qanun fil Tibb* (*The Canon of Medicine*). (*TCM*). Adapted by Laleh Bakhtiar, §487-§498; §500; §512-513; §527.

82 Avicenna. (1997). See *Qanun fil Tibb* (*The Canon of Medicine*). (TCM). Adapted by Laleh Bakhtiar, §447-§448; §476; §479; §480.

83 Avicenna. (1997). See *Qanun fil Tibb* (*The Canon of Medicine*). (*TCM*). Adapted by Laleh Bakhtiar, §450.

84 Avicenna. (1997). See *Qanun fil Tibb* (*The Canon of Medicine*). (*TCM*). Adapted by Laleh Bakhtiar, §451.

85 Avicenna. (1997). See *Qanun fil Tibb* (*The Canon of Medicine*). (*TCM*). Adapted by Laleh Bakhtiar, §57-§67.

86 Avicenna. (1997). See *Qanun fil Tibb* (*The Canon of Medicine*). (*TCM*). Adapted by Laleh Bakhtiar, §1414-§1438.

87 Avicenna. (1952). *Kitab al-Najat*, p. 25. Fazlur Rahman, (FR).

88 Avicenna. (1997). See *Qanun fil Tibb* (*The Canon of Medicine*). (*TCM*). Adapted by Laleh Bakhtiar, §454-§456.

89 Avicenna. (1997). See *Qanun fil Tibb* (*The Canon of Medicine*). (*TCM*). Adapted by Laleh Bakhtiar, §460-§476.

90 Avicenna. (1952). *Kitab al-Najat*, p. 24. Fazlur Rahman, (FR).

91 Avicenna. (1952). *Kitab al-Najat*, p. 26. Fazlur Rahman, (FR).

92 Avicenna. (1952). *Kitab al-Najat*, p. 28. Fazlur Rahman, (FR).

93 Avicenna. (1997). See *Qanun fil Tibb* (*The Canon of Medicine*). (*TCM*). Adapted by Laleh Bakhtiar, §458-§459.

94 Avicenna. (1952). *Kitab al-Najat*, p. 28. Fazlur Rahman, (FR).

95 Seyyed Hossein Nasr. (2001). (SCI), pp. 219-220.

96 Avicenna. (1952). *Kitab al-Najat*, p. 25. Fazlur Rahman, (FR).

97 Avicenna. (1952). *Kitab al-Najat*, pp. 25. Fazlur Rahman, (FR).

98 Avicenna. (1952). *Kitab al-Najat*, pp. 26. Fazlur Rahman, (FR).

99 Avicenna. (1952). *Kitab al-Najat*, pp. 27. Fazlur Rahman, (FR).

100 Avicenna. (1952). *Kitab al-Najat*, pp. 27. Fazlur Rahman, (FR).

101 Avicenna. (1952). *Kitab al-Najat*, pp. 27. Fazlur Rahman, (FR).

102 Avicenna. (1952). *Kitab al-Najat*, pp. 27. Fazlur Rahman, (FR).

103 Avicenna. (1997). See *Qanun fil Tibb* (*The Canon of Medicine*). (*TCM*). Adapted by Laleh Bakhtiar, §554-§556.

104 Avicenna. *Kitab al-Shifa*, pp. 33-34; *Kitab al-Najat*, p. 198. Syed Muhammad Naquib al-Attas, (*NHS*), p. 9.

105 Avicenna. (1952). *Kitab al-Najat*, pp. 30-32. Fazlur Rahman, (FR).

106 Avicenna. (1990) *Kitab al-Najat*, p. 200-201. Syed Muhammad Naquib al-Attas, (*NHS*), p. 10.

107 Avicenna. (1952). *Kitab al-Najat*, pp. 30-32. Fazlur Rahman, (FR).

108 Avicenna. (1952). *Kitab al-Najat*, pp. 30. Fazlur Rahman, (FR).

109 Syed Muhammad Naquib al-Attas. (1990). (*NHS*), pp. 12-13.

110 Avicenna. (1997). See *Qanun fil Tibb* (*The Canon of Medicine*). (*TCM*). Adapted by Laleh Bakhtiar, §564-§565.

111 Avicenna. (1997). See *Qanun fil Tibb* (*The Canon of Medicine*). (*TCM*).

Adapted by Laleh Bakhtiar, §560-§564.

112 Avicenna. (2010). *Kitab al-Shifa*, "Psychology", I.5, 43.1-44.3, See Jon McQinnis (JM), pp. 111-113.

113 Avicenna. (1997). *Kitab al-Shifa*, pp. 145-150, Syed Muhammad Naquib al-Attas, (*NHS*), p. 15.

114 Avicenna. (1997). *Kitab al-Najat*, pp. 219-220, Syed Muhammad Naquib al-Attas, (*NHS*), p. 31-32.

115 Avicenna. (1997). *Kitab al-Shifa,* pp. 39-40; *Kitab al-Najat*, p. 204, Syed Muhammad Naquib al-Attas, (*NHS*), p. 19-20.

116 Avicenna. (1990) *Kitab al-Shifa*, pp. 50-51; *Kitab al-Najat*, pp. 207-211. Syed Muhammad Naquib al-Attas (*NHS*), pp. 18-19.

117 Avicenna. (1952). *Kitab al-Najat*, p. 34. Fazlur Rahman, (FR).

118 Avicenna. (1990). *Kitab al-Shifa*, pp. 212-220. Syed Muhammad Naquib al-Attas, (*NHS*), p. 20-21.

119 Avicenna. (1990). *Kitab al-Shifa*, p. 208; *Kitab al-Najat*, p. 231. Syed Muhammad Naquib al-Attas, (*NHS*), p. 20-21.

120 Avicenna. (1952). *Kitab al-Najat*, p. 34. Fazlur Rahman, (FR).

121 Avicenna. (1990). *Kitab al-Najat*, p. 34. Fazlur Rahman, (FR), p. 20-21.

122 Avicenna. (1990). *Kitab al-Shifa*, pp. 39-40; *Kitab al-Najat*, p. 205. Syed Muhammad Naquib al-Attas, (*NHS*), p. 22.

123 Avicenna. (1952). *Kitab al-Najat*, p. 33-35. Fazlur Rahman, (FR).

124 Laleh Bakhtiar, translator. (2007). *The Sublime Quran*, 24:35.

125 Avicenna. (1958). *Kitab al-Isharat wal Tanbihat* (*The Book of Directives and Remarks*), pp. 364-367. Translated by Seyyed Hossein Nasr. (*SCI*), p. 96. Words in brackets are by the editor.

126 Syed Muhammad Naquib al-Attas. (1990). (*NHS*), pp. 34-35.

127 Avicenna. (1990). *Kitab al-Shifa*, p. 197; *Kitab al-Najat*, pp. 220-221. Syed Muhammad Naquib al-Attas, (*NHS*), p. 28.

128 Seyyed Hossein Nasr. (1976). (*ISIS*), p. 161.

129 Avicenna. (1997). See *Qanun fil Tibb* (*The Canon of Medicine*). (*TCM*). Adapted by Laleh Bakhtiar, §691-§694.

130 Avicenna. (1997). See *Qanun fil Tibb* (*The Canon of Medicine*). (*TCM*). Adapted by Laleh Bakhtiar, §1578-§1611.

131 Avicenna. (1997). See *Qanun fil Tibb* (*The Canon of Medicine*). (*TCM*). Adapted by Laleh Bakhtiar, §836-§840.

132 Avicenna. (1997). See *Qanun fil Tibb* (*The Canon of Medicine*). (*TCM*). Adapted by Laleh Bakhtiar, §789-§791; §1519-§1527.

133 Avicenna. (1997). See *Qanun fil Tibb* (*The Canon of Medicine*). (*TCM*). Adapted by Laleh Bakhtiar, §1552-§1553.

134 Avicenna. (1997). See *Qanun fil Tibb* (*The Canon of Medicine*). (*TCM*). Adapted by Laleh Bakhtiar, §792-§800.

135 Avicenna. (1997). See *Qanun fil Tibb* (*The Canon of Medicine*). (*TCM*). Adapted by Laleh Bakhtiar, §503-§513; §528.

136 Avicenna. (1997). See *Qanun fil Tibb* (*The Canon of Medicine*). (*TCM*). Adapted by Laleh Bakhtiar, §529-§535.

137 Avicenna. (1997). See *Qanun fil Tibb* (*The Canon of Medicine*). (*TCM*). Adapted by Laleh Bakhtiar, §514-§521.

138 Avicenna. (1997). See *Qanun fil Tibb* (*The Canon of Medicine*). (*TCM*). Adapted by Laleh Bakhtiar, §871-§873.

139 Avicenna. (1997). See *Qanun fil Tibb* (*The Canon of Medicine*). (*TCM*). Adapted by Laleh Bakhtiar, §874-§877.

140 Avicenna. (2010). *Kitab al-Shifa*, "Psychology", 1.5, 46:15-47.7; *Kitab al-Najat*, "Psychology", 3, 330-332. Jon McGinnis, (JM), p. 211.

141 Avicenna. (1991). *Rasail fil al-Ilm al-Akhlaq* (On the Science of Ethics) in *Rasail fi al-Hikmah wal-Tabiiyyat*, pp. 152-154. Majid Fakhry, *Ethical Theories in Islam* (MF), p 86.

142 Avicenna. (1991). *Rasail fil al-Ilm al-Akhlaq* (On the Science of Ethics) in *Rasail fi al-Hikmah wal-Tabiiyyat*, pp. 152-154. Majid Fakhry, (MF), p. 86.

143 Avicenna. (1991). *Fi al-Ahd* in *Rasail fi al-Hikmah wal-Tabiiyyat*, p. 145. Majid Fakhry, (MF), p. 87.

144 Majid Fakhry. (1991). *Ethical Theories in Islam*, p 85.

145 Avicenna. (1991). *Rasail fil Ilm al-Akhlaq* in *Rasail fil-Hikmah wal-Tabiiyyat.* Majid Fakhry, (MF), p 85.

146 Avicenna. (1991). *Risail fil al-Ahd* in *Rasail fil-Hikmah wal-Tabiiyyat*, p. 149. Majid Fakhry, (MF), p. 87.

147 Avicenna. (1991). *Rasail fil Ahd* in *Rasail fil-Hikmah wal-Tabiiyyat*, p. 145. Majid Fakhry, (MF), 86.

148 Avicenna. (1991). *Rasail fil Ahd* in *Rasail fil-Hikmah wal-Tabiiyyat*, p 145. Majid Fakhry, (MF), p. 86.

149 Avicenna. (1952). *Kitab al-Najat*, p. 32-33. Fazlur Rahman, (FR)

150 Jon McGinnis. (2010). *Avicenna*, p. 213.

151 Avicenna. (2010). *Kitab al-Shifa,* "Psychology", 354.16-17. Jon McGinnis, (JM), p. 213.

152 Avicenna, *Risalah fil Ilm al-Akhlaq* in *Tis Rasail fil Hikmah wal-Tabiiyyat*, p. 107. Majid Fakhry, (MF), p. 86.

153 Avicenna, *Risalah fil Ilm al-Akhlaq* in *Tis Rasail fil Hikmah wal-Tabiiyyat*, p. 107. Majid Fakhry, (MF), p. 86.

154 Avicenna, *Risalah fil Ilm al-Akhlaq* in *Tis Rasail fil Hikmah wal-Tabiiyyat*, p. 107. Majid Fakhry, (MF), p. 87.

155 Avicenna, *Risalah fil Ilm al-Akhlaq* in *Tis Rasail fil Hikmah wal-Tabiiyyat*, p. 107. Majid Fakhry, (MF), p. 87.

156 Avicenna. (1997). See *Qanun fil Tibb* (*The Canon of Medicine*). (*TCM*). Adapted by Laleh Bakhtiar, p. 535.

157 Avicenna, *Kitab al-Shifa,* "Psychology", V.1, 206.11-209.13. Jon McGinnis, (JM), pp. 212-213.

158 Avicenna, *Kitab al-Shifa*, Metaphysics, II, p. 445. See Jon McQuinnis, (JM), p. 215.

159 Avicenna, *Kitab al-Shifa*, Ilahiyat, p. 455. See Seyyed Hossein Nasr, (*ICD*), p. 203.

160 Mohammad Hashim Kamali. (2006) "Reading the Signs: A Quranic Per-

spective on Thinking," *Islam & Science,* Winter, Volume 4, Number 2.

161 William Chittick. (2007). *Science of the Cosmos, Science of the Soul* (WC), p. 5.

162 A. Okasha, C.R. (2001). "Mental Health and Psychiatry in the Middle East". *Eastern Mediterranean Health Journal* 7: 336–347.

163 Avicenna. (2010). *Kitab al-Shifa, "*Psychology", 1.1, 6. I. Jon McGinnis, (JM), p. 93.

164 Avicenna.(2006). *Kitab al-Shifa*, "Psychology", Ii. Lenn E. Goodman, (LG), p. 155-156

165 William Chittick. (2007). (WC), p. 32.

166 William Chittick. (2007). (WC), p. 31.

167 Avicenna. (2010). *Kitab al-Shifa*, "Psychology", V.5, 234.9- 13. Jon McGinnis, (JM), p. 131. Words in paranthesis are by the editor.

168 Avicenna, *Kitab al-Shifa*, "Psychology", V.5, 234.14-236.2. Jon McGinnis, (JM), pp. 131-132.

169 Avicenna. (2007) *Kitab al-Isharat wal Tanbihat*, vol. 3, p. 227. William Chittick, (WC), p. 123.

BIBLIOGRAPHY

PRIMARY SOURCES

Avicenna. (1906). *Qasida al-Ainiyya* (*Ode to the Soul*) II, pp. 110-111. Translated by E. G. Browne. *A Literary History of Persia* 4 vols. London: T. Fisher Unwin.

———(1326/1908). *Rasail Fi Ilm al-Akhlaq* in *Tis Rasail fi al-Hikmah wa al-Tabiyyat*. Cairo: Amin Hindiyyah.

———(1326/1908). *Tis Rasail Fil-Hikmah wal-Tabiyyat*. Cairo: Amin Hindiyyah.

———1326/1908). *Rasail Fil-Ahd* in *Tis Rasail Fil-Hikmah wal-Tabiyyat*. Cairo: Amin Hindiyyah.

———(1930). *Qanun fil Tibb: A Treatise on the Canon of Medicine by Avicenna, Incorporating a Translation of the First Book*. Translated by O. Cameron Gruner. London, UK: Luzac & Co.

———(1936). *Kitab al-Najat*. 2d ed. Cairo: Muhy al-Din Sabri al-Kurdi.

———(1951). *On Theology*. Translated by Arthur J. Arberry. CT: Hyperion Press.

———(1331-1951). *Risalah dar Haqiqat wa Kaifiyat-i Silsila-yi Mawjudat wa Tasalsul-i Asbab wa Musabbabat*. Edited by Musa Amid. Tehran: Anjuman-i-Athar-i Milli.

———(1331/1952). *Danishnamah-yi Ala al-Dawlah* (Book of Science Dedicated to Ala al-Dawlah), *Ilahiyat*. Edited by Muhammad Moin. Tehran: Anjuman-i Athar-i Milli.

———(1952). *Ahwal al-Nafs*. Edited by Ahmad Fuad al-Ahwani. Cairo: Isa al-babi al-Halabi.

———(1952). *Kitab al-Najat: Avicenna's Psychology: An English Translation of Kitab al-Najat, Book II, Chapter VI with Historico-Philosophical Notes and Textual Improvements on the Cairo Edition*. (FR) Translated by Fazlur Rahman. Oxford, UK: Oxford University Press.

———(1954). *Fil-Akhlaq wal-Infialat al-Nafsaniyyah*. Cairo: Publications de l'Institut Francais d'Archeologie Oriental.

———(1958). *Kitab al-Isharat wal-Tanbihat*. Edited by Sulayman Dunya. 4 parts in 3 vols. Cairo: Dar al-Maarif.

———(1959). *Kitab al-Nafs* in *Kitab al-Shifa: Physics VI*. Edited by F. Rahman. London: Oxford University Press.

———(1973). *Metaphysics* in *Kitab al-Shifa*. Translated by Parviz Morewedge. London: Routledge & Kegan Paul.

———(1982). *Kitab al-Isharat wal-Tanbihat*. Edited by J. Forget. Leiden: E. J. Brill.

———(1997). *Qanun fil-Tibb* (*The Canon of Medicine*) (*TCM*), vol. 1. Adapted by Laleh Bakhtiar from the translations of O. Cameron Gruner and Mazar H. Shah. Great Books of the Islamic World. Chicago, IL: KAZI Publications.

———(2005) *Kitab al-Shifa, Kitab al-Ilahiyat* (*Metaphysics of the Healing*). Translated by Michael E. Marmura with Arabic Edition. Provo, UT: Brigham

Young University Press.

———(2009). *Kitab al-Shifa, al-Tabiiyat*, as *Sama al-Tabii* (*Physics of the Healing*). Translated by Jon McGinnis with Arabic edition. Provo: Brigham Young University Press.

———(2012) *Qanun fil-Tibb* (*The Canon of Medicine: Natural Pharmaceuticals*), vol. 2. Compiled by Laleh Bakhtiar. Great Books of the Islamic World. Chicago, IL: KAZI Publications.

———(2012) *Qanun fil-Tibb* (*The Canon of Medicine*: *Natural Pharmaceuticals*, vol. 2, *On Cosmetics and their Medicinal Uses*). Compiled by Laleh Bakhtiar. Great Books of the Islamic World. Chicago, IL: KAZI Publications.

———(2012) *Qanun fil-Tibb* (*The Canon of Medicine*) (*TCM*), vol. 1, *On Diagnosis: Signs and Symptoms*. Adapted by Laleh Bakhtiar from translations by O. Cameron and Mazar H. Shah. Great Books of the Islamic World. Chicago, IL: KAZI Publications.

———(2012) *Qanun fil-Tibb* (*The Canon of Medicine*) (*TCM*), vol. 1, *On Diseases, Causes and Symptoms*. Adapted by Laleh Bakhtiar from translations by O. Cameron and Mazar H. Shah. Great Books of the Islamic World. Chicago, IL: KAZI Publications.

———(2012) *Qanun fil-Tibb* (*The Canon of Medicine*) (*TCM*), vol. 1, *On Healthy Living: Childbirth and Infancy*. Adapted by Laleh Bakhtiar from translations by O. Cameron and Mazar H. Shah. Great Books of the Islamic World. Chicago, IL: KAZI Publications.

———(2012) *Qanun fil-Tibb* (*The Canon of Medicine*) (*TCM*), vol. 1, *On Healthy Living: Exercising, Massaging, Bathing, Eating, Drinking, Sleeping and Treating Fatigue*. Adapted by Laleh Bakhtiar from translations by O. Cameron and Mazar H. Shah. Great Books of the Islamic World. Chicago, IL: KAZI Publications.

———(2012) *Qanun fil-Tibb* (*The Canon of Medicine*) (*TCM*), vol. 1, *On Healthy Living: Managing the Elderly, Temperament Extremes and Environmental Changes*. Adapted by Laleh Bakhtiar from translations by O. Cameron and Mazar H. Shah. Great Books of the Islamic World. Chicago, IL: KAZI Publications.

———(2012) *Qanun fil-Tibb* (*The Canon of Medicine*) (*TCM*), vol. 1, *On Medicine and Its Topics*. Adapted by Laleh Bakhtiar from translations by O. Cameron and Mazar H. Shah. Great Books of the Islamic World. Chicago, IL: KAZI Publications.

———(2012) *Qanun fil-Tibb* (*The Canon of Medicine*) (*TCM*), vol. 1, *On the Breath*. Adapted by Laleh Bakhtiar from translations by O. Cameron and Mazar H. Shah. Great Books of the Islamic World. Chicago, IL: KAZI Publications.

———(2012) *Qanun fil-Tibb* (*The Canon of Medicine*) (*TCM*), vol. 1, *On the Causes of Illness* (*Etiology*). Adapted by Laleh Bakhtiar from translations by O. Cameron and Mazar H. Shah. Great Books of the Islamic World. Chicago, IL: KAZI Publications.

———(2012) *Qanun fil-Tibb* (*The Canon of Medicine*) (*TCM*), vol. 1, *On the Four*

Elements. Adapted by Laleh Bakhtiar from translations by O. Cameron and Mazar H. Shah.

———(2012) *Qanun fil-Tibb* (*The Canon of Medicine*) (*TCM*), vol. 1, *On the Four Humours*. Adapted by Laleh Bakhtiar from translations by O. Cameron and Mazar H. Shah. Great Books of the Islamic World. Chicago, IL: KAZI Publications.

———(2012) *Qanun fil-Tibb* (*The Canon of Medicine*) (*TCM*), vol. 1, *On the Temperaments*. Adapted by Laleh Bakhtiar from translations by O. Cameron and Mazar H. Shah. Great Books of the Islamic World. Chicago, IL: KAZI Publications.

———(2012) *Qanun fil-Tibb* (*The Canon of Medicine*) (*TCM*), vol. 1, *On the Pulse*. Adapted by Laleh Bakhtiar from translations by O. Cameron and Mazar H. Shah. Great Books of the Islamic World. Chicago, IL: KAZI Publications.

———(2012) *Qanun fil-Tibb* (*The Canon of Medicine*) (*TCM*), vol. 1, *On the Three Faculties*. Adapted by Laleh Bakhtiar from translations by O. Cameron and Mazar H. Shah. Great Books of the Islamic World. Chicago, IL: KAZI Publications.

———(2012) *Qanun fil-Tibb* (*The Canon of Medicine*) (*TCM*), vol. 1, *On Therapeutics: Diseases, Disorders, Obstructions, Swellings and Managing Pain*. Adapted by Laleh Bakhtiar from translations by O. Cameron and Mazar H. Shah. Great Books of the Islamic World. Chicago, IL: KAZI Publications.

———(2012) Poem on Medicine (*Urjuza fil tibb*): *A Textbook on Traditional Medicine*. Adapted by Laleh Bakhtiar. Great Books of the Islamic World. Chicago, IL: KAZI Publications.

———(2012). *Qanun fil-Tibb* (*The Canon of Medicine*: *Natural Pharmaceuticals*, vol. 2, *On Aphrodisiacs and their Medicinal Uses*. Compiled by Laleh Bakhtiar. Great Books of the Islamic World. Chicago, IL: KAZI Publications.

———(2012). *Qanun fil-Tibb* (*The Canon of Medicine*: *Natural Pharmaceuticals*, vol. 2, *On the Healing Properties of Minerals, Plants, Herbs and Animals*. Compiled by Laleh Bakhtiar. Great Books of the Islamic World. Chicago, IL: KAZI Publications.

———(2012). *Qanun fil-Tibb* (*The Canon of Medicine*: *Natural Pharmaceuticals*, vol. 2, *On Treating Arthritis and the Joints*. Compiled by Laleh Bakhtiar. Great Books of the Islamic World. Chicago, IL: KAZI Publications.

———(2012). *Qanun fil-Tibb* (*The Canon of Medicine*: *Natural Pharmaceuticals*, vol. 2, *On Treating Swellings and Pimples*. Compiled by Laleh Bakhtiar. Great Books of the Islamic World. Chicago, IL: KAZI Publications.

———(2012). *Qanun fil-Tibb* (*The Canon of Medicine*: *Natural Pharmaceuticals*, vol. 2, *On Treating the Alimentary Organs and Diet*. Compiled by Laleh Bakhtiar. Great Books of the Islamic World. Chicago, IL: KAZI Publications.

———(2012). *Qanun fil-Tibb* (*Canon of Medicine*: *Natural Pharmaceuticals*, vol. 2, *On Treating the Excretory Organs*. Compiled by Laleh Bakhtiar. Great Books of the Islamic World. Chicago, IL: KAZI Publications.

———(2012). *Qanun fil-Tibb* (*The Canon of Medicine*: *Natural Pharmaceuticals*, vol. 2, *On Treating the Organs of the Head*. Compiled by Laleh Bakhtiar.

Great Books of the Islamic World. Chicago, IL: KAZI Publications.

————(2012). *Qanun fil-Tibb* (*The Canon of Medicine*: *Natural Pharmaceuticals*, vol. 2, *On Treating the Respiratory Organs and the Chest*. Compiled by Laleh Bakhtiar. Great Books of the Islamic World. Chicago, IL: KAZI Publications.

————(2012). *Qanun fil-Tibb* (*The Canon of Medicine*: *Natural Pharmaceuticals*, vol. 2, *On Treating the Visual Organs*. Compiled by Laleh Bakhtiar. Great Books of the Islamic World. Chicago, IL: KAZI Publications.

————(2012). *Qanun fil-Tibb* (*The Canon of Medicine*: *Natural Pharmaceuticals*, vol. 2, *On Treating Wounds and Ulcers*. Compiled by Laleh Bakhtiar. Great Books of the Islamic World. Chicago, IL: KAZI Publications.

————(2013). *On Cardiac Drugs*. Adapted by Laleh Bakhtiar. Great Books of the Islamic World. Chicago: KAZI Publications.

————(2013). *On the Science of the Soul*. Adapted by Laleh Bakhtiar. Great Books of the Islamic World. Chicago: KAZI Publications.

Rumi, Jalal al-Din. (1898). *Divan-e Shams-e Tabrizi* 3:218. Translated by R. A. Nicholson. Cambridge, UK: Cambridge University Press.

Rumi, Jalal al-Din. (1906). *Masnavi*, 3:218. Translated by E. G. Browne, *A Literary History of Persia*. 4 vols. London, UK: T. F. Unwin.

Shabistari, Mahmud. (1923). *Gulshan-i Raz* lines 250-255. Translated by E. H. Whinfield.

SECONDARY SOURCES

al-Attas, Syed Muhammad Naquib. (1990). *The Nature of Man and the Psychology of the Human Soul* (NHS), Kusala Lumpur, Malaysia: ISTAC.

Bakhtiar, Laleh. (1993). *Moral Healer's Handbook*. Chicago IL: Institute of Traditional Psychoethics and Guidance.

————(1993). *Moral Healing Through the Most Beautiful Names*. Chicago: Institute of Traditional Psychoethics and Guidance.

————(1993). *Traditional Psychoethics and Personality Paradigm*. Chicago IL: Institute of Traditional Psychoethics and Guidance.

————(2007). Translator of *The Sublime Quran*. Library of Islam. Chicago, IL: KAZI Publications.

Browne, E. G. (1906). *A Literary History of Persia*. 4 vols. London, UK: Luzac & Co.

Chittick, William. (2007). *Science of the Cosmos, Science of the Soul: The Pertinence of Islamic Cosmology in the Modern World* (WC). Oxford, UK: One World.

Corbin, Henri. (1960). *Avicenna and the Visionary Recitals*. Trasnlated by Willard R. Trask. Bollingen Series, v. 66. Princeton, NJ: Princeton University Press.

Davidson, Herbert. (1987) *Alfarabi, Avicenna, and Averroes, on Intellect*. New York and Oxford: Oxford University Press.

Druart, Therese-Anne. (1988) "The Soul and Body Problem: Avicenna and Descartes." In *Arabic Philosophy and the West*, ed. Therese-Anne Druart, 27-49. Washington, DC: Center for Contemporary Arab Studies, Georgetown

University.

Fakhry, Majid. (1991). *Ethical Theories in Islam* (MF). Leiden, Netherlands: E. J. Brill.

Goodman, Lenn E. (2006). *Avicenna* (LG). Ithaca, NY: Cornell University Press.

Hall, Robert E. (2004) "Intellect, Soul and Body in Ibn Sina: Systematic Synthesis and Development of the Aristotelian, Neoplatonic and Galenic Theories." In McGinnis, *Interpreting Avicenna*, 62-86

Hankinson, R. J. (2009). "Medicine and the Science of the Soul." *Can Bull Med Hist* 26(1):129-154.

Haque, Amber. (2004). "Psychology from an Islamic Perspective: Contributions of Early Muslim Scholars and Challenges to Contemporary Psychologists." *Journal of Religion and Health* (AH), 43(4):357-377.

Kamali, Mohammad Hashim. (2006). "Reading the Signs: A Quranic Perspective", *Islam & Science*, Winter, Volume 4, Number 2.

Lutz, Peter L. (2002). *The Rise of Experimental Biology: An Illustrated History.* New York, NY: Human Press.

Maher, Michael. (1982). *Psychology.* Bedford, MA: Magi Books.

McGinnis, Jon, ed. (2004) *Interpreting Avicenna: Science and Philosophy in Medieval Islam.* Leiden: E. J. Brill.

————(2010). *Avicenna.* (JM) Oxford, UK: Oxford University Press.

Nasr, Seyyed Hossein. (1976). *Islamic Science: An Illustrated Study* (*ISIS*). London, UK: World of Islam Festival.

————(1976). *Three Muslim Sages.* New York, NY: Caravan Books.

————and Oliver Leaman, eds. (1996). *History of Islamic Philosophy.* London and New York: Routledge.

————(1993). *An Introduction to Islamic Cosmological Doctrines* (*ICD*). Albany, NY: State University of New York Press.

————(2001). *Science and Civilization in Islam* (*SCI*). Chicago, IL: ABC International Group.

Okasha, A. C. R. (2001). "Mental Health and Psychiatry in the Middle East." *Eastern Mediterranean Health Journal* 7:336-347.

Sherif, Mohamed Ahmed. (1975). *Ghazali's Theory of Virtue.* Albany NY: State University of New York Press.

Yarsharter, Ehsan, ed. (1996-). *Encyclopedia Iranica*: Online Edition. New York, NY: Columbia Center for Iranian Studies.

INDEX

perception, 11, 56, 90
perceptive power, 15, 92, 94
perfection, 3, 11, 21, 64, 90, 98, 107
peristaltic movement, 26
phlegm, 28
physicians, 85
physics, 85, 107
place, 12
plant kingdom, 57
plant soul, 5-7, 46, 50
plastic power, 53
Platonic ideas, 62
pleasure, 57, 84, 86, 90
plethora, 81-82
position, 11-12
positive trait, 100
possible power, 63
potential intellect, 37
potential power, 63, 65
potherbs, 72, 74
power differentiation, 61
power of attraction, 40
practical intellect, 14-15, 61, 63, 69, 97-100
preservation of health, 43, 46
preserve shape or form, 46
primary matter, 67
primary perception, 55, 59
principles, first, 1
progressive change, 19
prophecy, 14
Prophet, 66, 103
prophetic inspiration, 14
prophets, 14
purslane, 73
qualitative pattern of organization, 17
qualitative, formal, 32
quality, 12
quantitative pattern of organization, 17
quantity, 1, 12
quickness of understanding, 13
Quran 24:35, 68
Quranic verses, 105
Radical Moisture, 21, 42-45, 89, 106

radio waves, 35
radish, 79
rancor, 92
rational imagination, 57, 61, 64
rational intellect, 9-10, 107
rational soul, 2, 9, 70, 100, 108
Real, the, 109
realization, 13
reason, 41, 62, 70, 88, 91, 97-98, 105
rectilinear form, 19
remembrance of God, 103
repletion, 73
reproduction, 3, 5, 40-41, 46, 51
resurrection, 103
retaining forms, 57-58
retention, 40, 47-48, 50-51, 93
ros, 42
rubies, 5
ruddy-yellow oxidized bile, 22
ruh, 28
sadness, 39, 90
sages, 85
salammoniac, 5
salts, 5
salty serous humour, 24
sanguineous humour, 21-22, 24, 40, 48
scammony, 10
secondary perception, 55, 59
seeing, 54, 57
self-aware, 109
self-awareness, 9, 108
self-preservation, 53
semen, 42
sensation, 64, 69, 88
sensation/perception 7, 39, 41, 53, 84
sense impressions, 60
sense-experience, 10
sense-imagery, 12
sense-organs, 61
sensible form(s), 56, 106
sensible images, 60
sensitive imagination, 57, 60
sensory nerves, 29
sero-atrabilious humour, 27

CPSIA information can be obtained
at www.ICGtesting.com
Printed in the USA
FSHW011124050621
81986FS